Word Perfect

vocabulary
for
fluency

MARK HARRISON

Nelson

Thomas Nelson and Sons Ltd
Nelson House Mayfield Road
Walton-on-Thames Surrey
KT12 5PL   UK

51 York Place
Edinburgh
EH1 3JD   UK

Thomas Nelson (Hong Kong) Ltd
Toppan Building 10/F
22A Westlands Road
Quarry Bay   Hong Kong

First published by Thomas Nelson and Sons Ltd 1990

ISBN 0-17-555873-6

NPN 9 8 7 6 5 4 3 2 1

Printed in Hong Kong

Contents _____

Contents

Introduction

Word Perfect is intended for intermediate and advanced level students of English who wish to acquire a level of vocabulary through which they can express themselves naturally in contemporary English. The book aims to increase students' ability to express thoughts and feelings, by providing a range of alternative words and expressions suitable for use in particular contexts. Such a range of expression is clearly essential to achieving fluency in any language.

Organisation

Word Perfect consists of 50 units which bring together words and expressions of similar meaning, of opposite meaning, or which are related in some other way. For example, the unit entitled '*Important/Trivial*' includes adjectives of similar meaning to '*important*' such as '*essential*' and '*crucial*', adjectives of opposite meaning, such as '*trivial*' and '*minor*', as well as related nouns, verbs and expressions such as '*a priority*', '*to stress*', '*to play down*', and '*so what?*' Each entry is followed by a definition and by examples which show the use of the word or phrase in context. Where a word has several different meanings, only those meanings related to the 'theme' of the unit are included. By grouping words together in this way, *Word Perfect* clarifies many areas of common confusion, and enables students to differentiate between words and phrases of related meaning, and to discriminate in terms of the appropriate context for use.

The 'reference' section of each unit is followed by a variety of practice exercises, the majority of them in the style of the Cambridge First Certificate and Proficiency examinations. These include multiple-choice, sentence-transformation, gap-fill and word-building exercises. Students can check their answers by referring to the answer key at the back of the book.

The units are grouped together into six sections: *Behaviour; Feelings and States of Mind; Characteristics; Thought, Knowledge and Ability; Communicating;* and *Doing and Causing.* These sections are meant more as a guide to where a particular 'subject' or notion can be found than as a strict categorisation.

The book also contains an index for easy reference, and an appendix of irregular verbs.

Ensuring accuracy

Each entry in *Word Perfect* includes the information which students need to be able to use the new items of vocabulary accurately. This information includes:

Prepositions

Knowing which preposition to use with a particular adjective, noun or verb is frequently a nightmare for non-native speakers of English. *Word Perfect* aims to solve this problem by indicating those prepositions which are most commonly used with a particular entry, and which students are therefore most likely to hear and need to use.

Verb patterns

Another common problem is knowing what type of grammatical construction follows a particular verb. *Word Perfect* tells the student whether a verb is followed by a direct object, by a gerund or infinitive, by a '*that*' clause, or by a combination of two or more of these features. For example:

to ignore (s.o./sth) – direct object
to feel like (sth/*doing* sth) – direct object or gerund
to manage (*to do* sth) – infinitive
to ensure (*that ...*) – '*that*' clause

Countable or uncountable?

Whether a noun is countable or uncountable is indicated by the use or omission of the indefinite article ('a' or 'an') in the entry. For example:

a rip-off – countable
an apology – countable
guilt – uncountable

In some cases, a noun may have both countable and uncountable functions, and this is shown by its inclusion in both forms. For example:

luxury – uncountable
a luxury – countable

Both forms are not always included, if one form is used less frequently than the other.

Collocations

Words often tend to 'collocate' or be used in combination with certain other words. In order to sound natural and achieve fluency in English, the non-native speaker must be familiar with collocations. *Word Perfect* therefore includes many examples of collocations. For example '*luck*' is followed by '*a stroke of luck*', '*a complaint*' by '*to make a complaint*', and other collocations are included in their own right, for example '*to bear a grudge*', '*on average*', and '*by chance*'. If you said 'by average' or 'through chance' you would probably be understood, but you would not sound natural.

How to use the book

The clarity of the definitions and examples, and the inclusion of an answer key to the exercises, make *Word Perfect* ideal for self-study. You can work through each unit in sequence, or you can use the contents page or index to choose a unit which interests you. Study the 'reference'

section of the unit carefully, paying particular attention to any grammatical features associated with an entry. Reading the examples and seeing the new item of vocabulary in context will help you further to understand when and how it is used. Ideally, the practice exercises should not be done immediately afterwards, since the aim is to be able to produce the vocabulary at any time, and the exercises should not simply be a short-span memory test. When you have done the exercises, check your answers with the answer key, referring back to the reference section if you have made any mistakes.

You do not of course have to do the exercises, and *Word Perfect* is very useful as a reference book. The inclusion of an index means that you can look up a word that you don't know, or clarify for yourself a particular problem such as the difference between '*remember*' and '*remind*'.

Word Perfect can also be used for exam preparation, to build vocabulary of the kind required for the Cambridge First Certificate and Proficiency examinations.

Section A
Behaviour

Units 1-9

Unit 1 Active/Sociable/Passive/Reserved _____

Part 1

1 **active**
doing a lot of things; always busy

She's very active and plays a lot of sport./Despite his age, he's still quite active.

2 **energetic**
full of energy

She leads a very energetic life – she gets up early and works very hard until late.

3 **lively**
full of life and energy

She was very lively tonight – she talked a lot and danced a lot.

4 **dynamic**
full of energy and ideas; having a powerful personality

She's a very dynamic woman and has become successful very quickly.

5 **sociable**
friendly; enjoying the company of other people

They're very sociable and like going to parties and spending time with other people.

6 **outgoing**
very friendly; always interested in meeting new people and doing new things

He's a very outgoing sort of person and has got lots of friends.

7 **talkative**
liking or willing to talk a lot

It's very difficult to have a conversation with him because he's not very talkative.

8 **decisive**
able to make decisions quickly and with certainty

You should be more decisive – you take too long to make up your mind.

9 **an extrovert**
a lively, sociable person who finds it easy to talk to people and likes to attract attention

He's an extrovert – when he's with other people he's often the centre of attention.

10 **to be good company**
to be an interesting and amusing person to be with

She's good company – she's always got a good story to tell.

Part 2

1 **passive**
not active; accepting what happens to you without trying to change or influence it

His reaction was passive – although he didn't like the situation, he didn't argue.

2 **lazy**
disliking activity; without the energy or interest to do anything

He doesn't like his job but he's too lazy to look for another one.

3 **apathetic**
completely unenthusiastic or
uninterested; having no desire to
change a bad situation

*She tried to organise a strike but the others were too
apathetic to join her.*

4 **quiet**
not saying very much

*Although she's quiet, it doesn't mean that she doesn't have
strong opinions.*

5 **reserved**
not saying what you think or feel

She's reserved and even if she's angry she doesn't say so.

6 **subdued**
less talkative than usual

*He normally has a lot to say but he was rather subdued
last night – I wonder if there's something wrong.*

7 **an introvert**
someone who is more interested
in their own thoughts and feelings
than in the world around them

*If she wasn't such an introvert she would make friends
more easily.*

Part 3

1 **to act**
to do something positive about a
problem to try to solve it

*The situation is getting worse – you must act now, before
it's too late.*

2 **initiative**
the ability to act and make
decisions without help from other
people

*She shows great initiative and is a good candidate for
promotion.*

3 **to use your initiative**
to act without help from others,
using your own judgement

*Why should I always have to tell you what to do? Use
your initiative for once.*

4 **to do something** (*about* sth)
to take action in an attempt to
solve a problem

*I can't just ignore the problem – I'll have to do something
about it./The Government have promised to do something
about the state of the roads.*

5 **to make up your mind**
to decide

*Make up your mind what you want to do – I can't wait
forever for an answer.*

6 **to have go**
to have energy

If you had a bit more go, you wouldn't be so bored.

7 **to be on the go**
to be very busy and active

I must sit down. I've been on the go all day.

8 **to liven up**
(of a person) to become more lively after being tired or without energy; (of an event) to become more interesting and exciting

I feel a bit tired at the moment but I'm sure I'll liven up later in the evening./The party livened up after about 11 o'clock when more people arrived.

9 **to hang about/around**
to stay in a place doing nothing, simply passing the time

They've got nothing to do so they hang about on street corners all the time./We had to hang around at the airport because the plane was delayed.

10 **to stand around**
to stand and do nothing

Everybody else stood around while I did all the work.

Unit 1 Exercises

1.1 *Choose the word or phrase (A, B, C or D) which best completes each sentence.*

1 He's so .... that he always expects other people to do the work.
A reserved B lazy C apathetic D passive

2 She's not very .... She's never quite sure what she wants to do.
A energetic B lively C active D decisive

3 Even though they don't agree with what's happening, they're too .... to protest.
A outgoing B subdued C quiet D apathetic

4 He wasn't very .... tonight. In fact he hardly said anything.
A active B decisive C talkative D energetic

5 I'm sure he enjoyed the evening. He didn't say much because he's .... by nature.
A passive B subdued C inactive D quiet

6 He's always been very .... so he hates not being able to do anything now that he's ill.
A decisive B active C outgoing D loud

7 I don't feel .... enough to go for a walk now.
A energetic B extrovert C outgoing D sociable

8 He's a .... sort of person. He doesn't really care what happens to him.
A quiet B passive C reserved D subdued

9 The school has just appointed a(n) .... new headmaster, whose job it will be to improve falling standards of education.
A sociable B active C dynamic D lively

10 It's always difficult to know what she's thinking because she's so ....
A apathetic B inactive C subdued D reserved

11 The job involves working closely with the public, so we're looking for someone with a(n) .... personality.
A talkative B outgoing C dynamic D active

12 I had to .... before the situation got worse.
A act B do something about C have go D be on the go

13 She hasn't got enough .... to really try to get what she wants.
   A action   B activity   C go   D decision

14 They're very .... and regularly invite people to their house.
   A good company   B lively   C active   D sociable

15 He seemed rather .... Was he upset about something?
   A unsocial   B apathetic   C passive   D subdued

16 She's very .... She can't sit down for long.
   A lively   B decisive   C impassive   D good company

17 Things are never boring when he's there. You could say he's ....
   A energetic   B active   C sociable   D an extrovert

18 She's .... She tends to think a lot and not to say a lot.
   A an introvert   B inverted   C inturned   D subdued

19 The successful candidate must have ...., as he or she will have to work without
   supervision.
   A action   B a go   C initiative   D decision

1.2   *Fill each of the blanks with one suitable word.*

1 Don't keep asking other people what to do. .... your initiative!

2 We just hung .... in the park because we had nothing else to do.

3 They're really .... company. I always enjoy spending an evening with them.

4 Do you want it or not? Come on, ... up your mind.

5 Make sure you're not late. I don't want to have to stand .... waiting for you.

6 The party was rather boring at the start, but everyone livened .... later.

7 The problem won't just go away. You'll have to do something .... it.

8 She's always .... the go. I don't know where she gets her energy from.

Unit 2 Careful/Conscientious/Careless/Impulsive _____

Part 1

1 **careful**
taking care (in order to avoid loss, damage, danger, mistakes etc.)
a (*with* sth)

Be careful with that vase, will you? It's worth a lot of money./He's very careful with his money, in fact some people say he's mean.

b (*of* s.o./sth, especially something that may harm you)

Be careful of the traffic when you cross the road./My mother always told me to be careful of strangers.

c (*to do* sth/*that* ...)

I was careful to choose the right words, so that they wouldn't misunderstand me./Be careful that you don't fall./ Be careful how you cross the road.

2 **cautious**
very careful; not wanting to act quickly, in order to avoid possible danger or bad results

He's cautious about accepting the offer before he knows all the details.

3 **wary** (*of* s.o./sth; *of doing* sth)
very cautious because you are not sure about something

After her divorce she was wary of getting involved with anyone again./He's very wary of people in authority.

4 **conscientious**
careful to do your work well

She's so conscientious that she often works late without getting paid.

5 **thorough**
careful in your work; paying attention to every detail

She's very thorough whenever she writes a report./The doctor gave him a thorough examination.

6 **efficient**
working well and quickly

They're an efficient company with a very good reputation.

7 **competent**
able to do a job well

He's a competent teacher and his students are making good progress.

8 **particular** (*about* sth)
not easily satisfied; choosing very carefully

She's particular about her food and there are some things she'll never eat.

9 **fussy** (*about* sth)
very particular

He's fussy about the clothes he buys and always takes ages to choose them.

Note: **I'm not fussy** = I don't mind

'Where would you like to sit?' – 'I'm not fussy.'

10 **conservative**
not wanting to do or try anything new or unusual

She's very conservative in her choice of clothes.

11 **to take care** (*of* s.o./sth)
to keep someone or something
safe and well or in good condition

If you take care of your records, they will last you for years./Who's going to take care of the children while you're on holiday?

12 **to look after** (s.o./sth)
to take care of

You should look after your health./Look after yourself!

13 **to mind** (sth/*that ...*)
(often used in the imperative) to
be careful of something

Mind the step!/Mind what you're doing with that knife!/ Mind (that) you don't fall!

14 **to watch out** (*for* sth)
to be very careful (to avoid
something which might be
dangerous)

Watch out or you'll get hurt./While you're in London, watch out for pickpockets.

15 **to look out** (*for* sth)
to be careful to notice

Look out for the hospital – that's where we have to turn right.

16 **to keep your eyes open** (*for* s.o./
sth)
to keep looking or watching (in
order to notice someone or
something)

I'm keeping my eyes open for another job, as I don't like the one I've got.

17 **to check** (sth/*that ...*)
to look again in order to see if
something is correct

I'll check the train timetable before I go, in case it's changed./Check (that) you haven't forgotten anything.

18 **to make sure** (*of* sth/*that ...*)
to check in order to be certain

Make sure (that) you haven't forgotten anything./Make sure of your facts before you accuse him.

19 **to ensure** (*that ...*)
(*formal*) to make sure

I repeated it to ensure that they'd heard me.

20 **to take a lot of trouble** (*over* sth)
to spend a lot of time and effort
doing something

This is a very exotic meal – you must have taken a lot of trouble over it.

21 **to protect** (s.o./sth *from/against*
s.o./sth)
to keep someone or something
safe from harm or danger

She wore a coat to protect herself from the cold./The children were vaccinated to protect them against disease.

Part 2

1 **careless** (*with/about* sth)
not careful; not paying attention to
what you do

He's a very careless driver./She's careless with money and frequently gets into debt./He's very careless about his appearance.

2 **sloppy**
doing work in a careless and
inadequate way

The painters were very sloppy and the room looks terrible.

3 **inefficient**
not efficient

*She's so inefficient that everybody else has to do her job
for her.*

4 **incompetent**
not competent

*He's really incompetent and does even the simplest jobs
badly.*

5 **impulsive**
acting suddenly without thinking

*I know it was impulsive of me, but I saw it and liked it so
much that I went straight into the shop and bought it./
She's impulsive and buys things she can't afford.*

6 **rash**
impulsive; doing foolish or
dangerous things

*It's rash to agree to do something you can't possibly do./It
was rather rash of them to buy the house without seeing it
first.*

7 **hasty**
acting or deciding too quickly

*Don't be too hasty! Think carefully about what might
happen.*

8 **spontaneous**
(of an event) not planned

*The party was completely spontaneous – we only decided
that evening to have one.*

9 **on the spur of the moment**
suddenly; without being planned

*On the spur of the moment I phoned a friend and
arranged to go out.*

10 **to jump to conclusions**
to make a judgement quickly and
without knowing all the facts

*Don't jump to conclusions! Just because he looks stupid, it
doesn't mean that he is.*

11 **a snap decision**
a sudden decision, made without
thinking carefully

*I didn't have time to think about it, I had to make a snap
decision.*

Unit 2 Exercises

2.1 *Choose the word or phrase (A, B, C or D) which best completes each sentence.*

1 I wouldn't say he was brilliant at his job, but he's quite ....
  A cautious   B wary   C effective   D competent

2 I'm .... trusting him again. He let me down last time.
  A wary of   B careful about   C conservative about   D conscientious of

3 You're too .... You should think before you act.
  A unconscious   B sloppy   C spontaneous   D impulsive

4 I'm very .... things. I'm always losing them.
  A careless about   B impulsive with   C careless of   D careless with

5 Don't make a .... decision. Think about it first.
A snap B jump C careless D spontaneous

6 I think you should be .... Find out exactly what they want you to do before you agree.
A defensive B cautious C fussy D conscientious

7 She lost her job because she was .... She made far too many mistakes.
A rash B inefficient C incautious D impulsive

8 The police made a .... search of the area but found nothing.
A wary B cautious C fussy D thorough

9 Be .... those glasses! Don't break them!
A careful about B careful of C careful with D particular about

10 I realise now that I was too .... I should have thought about it for longer.
A hasty B careless C snap D sloppy

11 He's really .... He never checks his work and it's always full of mistakes.
A snap B impulsive C rash D sloppy

12 I reminded him twice, so as to .... that he wouldn't forget.
A take care B watch out C make sure D check

13 .... your work in case you've made any mistakes.
A Take care of B Ensure C Look out for D Check

14 He's .... He does his job very badly.
A incompetent B rash C unconscious D hasty

15 We didn't plan the celebration. It was ....
A impulsive B rash C hasty D spontaneous

16 Be .... that step. It's broken and you might fall.
A careful of B careful about C cautious about D careful with

17 I'll send the letter today to .... that they receive it in time.
A take care B ensure C insure D protect

18 I never know what to cook him as he's such a .... eater. He doesn't even like potatoes.
A thorough B conservative C fussy D careful

19 She's very .... She takes her job very seriously.
A particular B conservative C conscientious D fussy

20 It was very .... of you to lose that letter; you should have kept it in a safe place.
A rash B impulsive C fussy D careless

21 I'm phoning them again because I want to .... the arrangements for tomorrow.
A ensure B make sure C make sure of D take care

22 You're so .... ! Can't you see the benefits of building the new road?
A hasty B thorough C conservative D fussy

23 Don't be .... ! It's a bad idea to phone them while you're angry. Wait until you've calmed down.
   A sloppy   B spontaneous   C rash   D careless

24 She's very .... She can be relied on to do her job properly.
   A efficient   B cautious   C serious   D conservative

25 I'm not .... I don't mind at all where we go.
   A careful   B cautious   C wary   D fussy

2.2   *For each of the sentences below, write a new sentence as similar as possible in meaning to the original sentence, but using the word given. This word must not be altered in any way.*

   EXAMPLE   It's no use arguing: I've made up my mind.
   point

   ANSWER   *There's no point in arguing; I've made up my mind.*

1 Look after yourself.
   care

   ....

2 Be careful of thieves if you go to that part of town.
   watch

   ....

3 I put a lot of care and attention into this letter.
   trouble

   ....

4 I've installed an alarm to stop thieves stealing my car.
   protect

   ....

5 I bought it without thinking about it first.
   spur

   ....

6 You're making a judgement before you've heard the facts.
   conclusions

   ....

7 I choose very carefully who I discuss my private life with.
   particular

   ....

8 I made sure that I didn't offend them.
   careful

   ....

9 I'll look for you at the concert, although I expect it will be very crowded.
   eyes

   ....

10 She chooses the kind of hotels she stays in very carefully.
fussy

....

11 Will you take care of the flat while I'm away?
look

....

12 Be careful not to hit your head.
mind

....

13 I don't mind whether we go or not.
fussy

....

14 Be careful to notice a red door when you arrive – that's my flat.
look

....

Unit 3 Honest/Truthful

1 **honest**

   a (of a person) able to be trusted because of not lying, cheating etc.

   Sandra is hard-working and honest, and I have no hesitation in recommending her for the job.

   b (of a person's behaviour or appearance) showing the qualities of an honest person

   He's got an honest face./I suspect that his motives are not entirely honest.

   c concerned only with the truth; not hiding anything

   Be honest. Tell me what you really think./If I'm honest with myself, the only reason I'm doing this job is for the money./I'm sorry if you don't like what I'm saying, but it's my honest opinion.

2 **trustworthy**
   (of a person) able to be trusted

   Shall we tell him our secret? Is he trustworthy enough?

3 **reliable**
   (of a person or thing) able to be relied on

   I doubt if he'll come – he's not particularly reliable./Don't believe everything you read – the newspapers are not always entirely reliable.

4 **the truth**
   something that is true; the facts

   The truth is I've never liked him./Nobody will ever know the truth of the matter.

5 **to tell the truth**

   Believe me, I'm telling the truth.

6 **truthful**

   a (of a statement etc.) true and honest

   I don't think that's an entirely truthful answer.

   b (of a person) telling the truth; honest

   Be truthful. Do you like my new suit or not?

7 **sincere**

   a (of a person) believing or meaning what you say (especially when saying nice things)

   She's very sincere, so if she says she likes you, you can be sure she does.

   b (of feelings etc.) truly and deeply felt

   Please accept our sincere apologies for the misunderstanding.

8 **genuine**
   sincere; really what it appears to be

   She's making a genuine effort to be more friendly./He gave me a look of genuine surprise.

9 **open**
   willing to discuss (often private) matters honestly

   She's always very open about her relationships.

10 **frank**
honest and open in expressing
your real thoughts and feelings
(even if the other person may not
like them)

She was completely frank with him – either he worked harder or he would be out of a job./He made a frank admission of guilt.

11 **direct**
honest and going straight to the
point, without hesitation

He was very direct and wasted no time in asking me if I was married./I expect a direct answer from you – do you or do you not know this man?

12 **blunt**
speaking directly, without trying
to be polite or hide your true
opinion, even if what you have to
say is unpleasant

I'm going to be blunt with you – if you go on like this, you'll never pass your exams./Don't be put off by her blunt manner – she's actually quite nice.

13 **to tell you the truth**
an expression used to admit
something and make it clear that
you are being honest and open

To tell you the truth, I think you've made a terrible mistake./I've forgotten his name, to tell you the truth.

14 **to be honest**
an expression meaning 'to tell you
the truth'

To be honest, we had an absolutely awful holiday./ Although I was pleasant to her, to be honest I can't stand her.

15 **honestly**
speaking truthfully (an expression
used to make it clear that what
you are saying is true, even if the
person you are talking to may not
believe it)

Honestly, it's not my fault that I'm late./I can't honestly say I care who wins./'I think you won by cheating.' – 'I didn't, honestly. I was just lucky.'

16 **frankly**
an expression used to make it
clear that what you are saying is
true, even though the person you
are talking to may not like it

Frankly, you're wasting your time trying to learn German, as you've obviously got no gift for languages.

17 **to be frank**
an expression meaning 'frankly'

He's got his driving test next week, but to be frank he doesn't stand a chance of passing.

18 **to speak your mind**
to say what you really think, not
what people want to hear

If I spoke my mind, he'd only get upset.

Unit 3 Exercises

3.1 *Choose the word or phrase (A, B, C or D) which best completes each sentence.*

1 He's very .... about his private life. He's got no secrets.
   A trustworthy   B direct   C open   D sincere

2 She was very .... and told me quite simply that she didn't like me.
   A genuine   B open   C blunt   D sincere

3 I don't think she was being completely .... when she said she liked my paintings.
   A frank   B sincere   C reliable   D true

4 If you were .... , you'd admit that it was your fault.
   A genuine   B true   C frank   D honest

5 He's got a very .... manner, so don't be surprised if, the first time you meet him, he asks you how much you earn.
   A sincere   B frank   C direct   D reliable

6 I'm writing to express my .... gratitude for all your help.
   A truthful   B blunt   C sincere   D honest

7 It was a .... mistake. I wasn't trying to cheat you.
   A genuine   B sincere   C truthful   D frank

8 I know you think it was me who told him your secret but .... , it wasn't.
   A honestly   B frankly   C to be honest   D to be frank

9 I've been completely .... Everything I've told you is what really happened.
   A true   B truthful   C genuine   D direct

10 I'm going to be .... with you, Mr Henderson. Your daughter is a thief.
   A sincere   B open   C frank   D genuine

3.2 *For each of the sentences below, write a new sentence as similar as possible in meaning to the original sentence, but using the word given. This word must not be altered in any way.*

EXAMPLE   It's no use arguing: I've made up my mind.
          point

ANSWER   *There's no point in arguing; I've made up my mind.*

1 You're lying.
  truth

   ....

2 The truth is that I didn't understand a word he said.
  honest

   ....

3 Can we trust her?
  trustworthy

   ....

4 My honest opinion is that you're wasting your time.
  frank

   ....

5 He's never afraid to say what he thinks.
mind

....

6 The witness can be relied on completely.
reliable

....

7 To be honest, I couldn't care less what you think.
tell

....

8 The truth is that there's no easy solution to your problems.
frankly

....

Unit 4 Dishonest/Deceitful

1 **dishonest**
not honest

He accused me of being dishonest./The Government has acted in a most dishonest way.

2 **deceitful**
behaving in a dishonest way by trying to hide the truth or make other people believe something that is not true

Don't you think you're being rather deceitful by not mentioning that you spent two years in prison?

3 **crooked**
dishonest, especially in a criminal way and in connection with money or business

Don't get involved with him – he's crooked./I don't know how he manages to earn so much money, but you can be sure it involves something crooked.

4 **untrustworthy**
not trustworthy

He's completely untrustworthy. In fact anything you tell him he's likely to use against you.

5 **unreliable**
not reliable

She's so unreliable. That's the third time she's kept me waiting this week./I don't know why they bother to print these bus timetables – they're completely unreliable.

6 **insincere**
not sincere

She was so obviously being insincere when she said she liked your paintings.

7 **two-faced**
behaving in an insincere way by saying one thing at one time or to one person, and the opposite thing at another time or to another person

How two-faced can you get! Only yesterday he told me how well I was doing and today he's been telling everyone that I'm useless.

8 **devious**
dishonest, especially in a complicated, clever or indirect way

He was prepared to use any means, no matter how devious, to secure the contract.

9 **cunning**
clever in using people and situations in order to get what you want (without them realising); cleverly deceitful

Reducing income tax just before the election was a cunning move by the government to get themselves re-elected.

10 **to lie** (*to s.o. about* sth)
to say something which you know is untrue

She's lying – it was her that broke the window, not me./'I've never seen him before,' she lied./I'm sure he's lying about his age. He must be at least forty./Don't ever lie to me again.

11 **a lie**
a deliberately untrue statement

That's a lie and you know it!/Don't believe what they're saying about me. It's all lies.

12 **to tell a lie**

No one trusts him because he's always telling lies.

13 **a liar**
a person who tells lies

*If he's saying that the accident was my fault, he's a liar./
You liar! You know that's not true.*

14 **to deceive** (s.o. *into doing* sth)
to cause someone to believe
something that is not true,
especially when it is for your own
advantage

*He deceived her with promises of marriage./She deceived
him into thinking she loved him, but we all knew it was
his money that she was after.*

15 **deceptive**
not as it appears to be

He may look honest, but appearances are often deceptive.

16 **to trick** (s.o. *into doing* sth/s.o.
out of sth)
to deceive someone, especially in
order to get something from them
or to cause them to do something

*They arrived at their destination only to find they had been
tricked – there was no luxury villa, no swimming pool, not
even the promised hire car./She realised that she had been
tricked into selling her house for far less than it was
really worth.*

17 **a trick**
something that is done in order to
trick someone

*Pretending to be ill was just a trick to get the day off
work./Is this a genuine offer, or just another one of your
tricks?*

18 **to cheat**
 a to behave in a dishonest way in
order to get what you want
(especially in games, examinations
etc.)

*Don't play cards with him – he cheats./The only way she's
going to pass her exam now is by cheating.*

 b (s.o. *out of* sth)
to trick someone into giving you
something

*He cheated her out of her savings by pretending he
worked for an investment company./They tried to cheat me
by charging me for fifteen lessons and only giving me ten.*

19 **a cheat**
a person who cheats

*Stop copying me, you cheat!/Don't let him keep the score
because he's a cheat.*

20 **to mislead** (s.o. *into doing* sth)
to give someone a wrong idea,
either intentionally or
unintentionally, causing them to
believe something that is not true

*The brochure misled us into thinking that our hotel was
only five minutes from the beach. Five minutes by
helicopter, perhaps!/Don't be misled by his charm.*

21 **misleading**
(of a statement etc.) causing you
to be misled

*It's a rather misleading advertisement, as it's not really a
free offer.*

22 **to fool** (s.o. *into doing* sth)
to deceive or trick someone

*He doesn't fool me. I know he's lying./She fooled me into
trusting her – how could I have been so stupid?*

23 **to con** (s.o. *into doing* sth/s.o. *out of* sth)
(*colloquial*) to trick someone, especially in order to get money from them

He conned me into buying a car that doesn't even work!/ They conned us out of £100.

24 **a con**
(*colloquial*) a trick, especially to get money

Don't send them any money before you receive the goods. The whole thing might be a con.

25 **to rip** (s.o.) **off**
(*colloquial*) to cheat someone by charging too much money for something

It's so obvious that most of the cafes here are just trying to rip off the tourists./A £20 taxi fare for a two-mile journey? You've been ripped off!

26 **a rip-off**
(*colloquial*) an example of being charged too much money for something, so that you feel cheated

What a rip-off! A hamburger here is double the price of one anywhere else.

27 **to do** (s.o.) **out of** (sth)
(*colloquial*) to cause someone to lose something, by cheating them

He did me out of £200./She feels that she's been done out of the job that should have been hers, because they preferred to appoint a man.

28 **to be taken in** (*by* sth)
to be deceived into believing something

Their story sounded so convincing that we were all taken in (by it).

29 **to fall for** (sth)
to be deceived into believing something, especially naively

I can't believe I fell for such a ridiculous hard luck story.

Unit 4 Exercises

4.1 *Choose the word or phrase (A, B, C or D) which best completes each sentence.*

1 I think he's .... I think he sells stolen goods.
A insincere   B false   C crooked   D deceitful

2 It was .... of you to lie to me about where you were last night.
A misleading   B false   C deceptive   D deceitful

3 She's so .... One minute she's your best friend, and the next minute she doesn't want to know you.
A deceptive   B two-faced   C deceitful   D misleading

4 He was very .... He flattered me so that I wouldn't be able to refuse him the favour he wanted.
A crooked   B two-faced   C cunning   D deceptive

5 She's .... If you tell her a secret, she tells other people.
   A deceitful   B insincere   C untrustworthy   D two-faced

6 The way he got me to do his work for him, without me realising what was really happening, was very ....
   A devious   B misleading   C crooked   D false

7 I'm not taken in by his .... praise.
   A dishonest   B two-faced   C deceitful   D insincere

8 Don't expect him to turn up on time. He's very ....
   A untrustworthy   B unreliable   C deceitful   D cunning

9 It's .... of you to say that. You know it isn't true.
   A dishonest   B devious   C untrustworthy   D false

10 I was .... by his honest appearance. Only later did I discover that he was a liar.
   A misled   B deviated   C done   D cheated

11 This photo of the house is rather .... It makes it look much bigger than it really is.
   A deceitful   B deceptive   C devious   D dishonest

12 Before you send them any money, make sure the company really exists. The whole thing could be a ....
   A deceit   B fool   C cheat   D con

13 I didn't think he'd .... such a pathetic lie, but he believed every word of it.
   A take up   B fall out   C take in   D fall for

14 You can't .... me! I know that story isn't true.
   A lie   B fool   C do   D cheat

15 I realise now that you've been .... me. You haven't been going out with your friends, you've been seeing another man.
   A lying   B doing   C deceiving   D conning

16 Their brochure is full of .... information. For example it says that all rooms are 'with shower', but it doesn't say that in some cases the shower is halfway down the corridor.
   A misleading   B deceptive   C deceitful   D insincere

17 This isn't a .... , is it? If I lend you my car, you will bring it back, won't you?
   A cheat   B trick   C rip-off   D deceit

4.2   *Fill each of the blanks with one suitable word.*

1 Have you seen the price of these jeans? What a .... -off!

2 He lied .... where he had really been that evening.

3 He's a .... What he's saying about me is totally untrue.

4 You .... ! You're not supposed to look at my cards in the middle of the game.

5 That's a .... ! I most certainly did not say I would lend you any money.

4.3 *For each of the sentences below, write a new sentence as similar as possible in meaning to the original sentence, but using the word given. This word must not be altered in any way.*

EXAMPLE   It's no use arguing: I've made up my mind.
point

ANSWER   *There's no point in arguing; I've made up my mind.*
....

1 Because I believed his lies, I paid far too much for it.
conned

....

2 Why aren't you telling me the truth?
lying

....

3 Because I believed her lies, I gave her £10.
tricked

....

4 I didn't tell the truth because I didn't want to say what had really happened.
lie

....

5 They cheated me.
ripped

....

6 When I checked my change, I realised I'd been deliberately charged £5 more than I should have been.
done

....

7 Because I believed his lies, he got a lot of money from me.
conned

....

8 He deliberately took £20 more from me than he should have done.
cheated

....

9 You didn't believe his story, did you?
taken

....

Unit 5 Kind/Grateful/Unkind/Selfish _____

Part 1

1 **kind** (*to* s.o.)
friendly and helpful; doing nice things for other people

She's always been very kind to me and has done a lot for me./It was kind of you to help me.

2 **kindness**
the quality of being kind

Her kindness helped me a lot when I was ill.

3 **considerate** (*towards* s.o.)
aware of the feelings or wishes of other people; kind

He's very considerate towards his friends – he always tries to help if one of them has a problem.

4 **consideration** (*for* s.o.)
thought for the feelings or wishes of other people

If he had more consideration for her she wouldn't be so unhappy, but he never thinks about her.

5 **thoughtful**
considerate

It was thoughtful of you to phone me while I was ill.

6 **sympathetic** (*to/towards* s.o.)
kind, and understanding of the feelings and problems etc. of other people

When I explained my problem he was very sympathetic./ She gave him a sympathetic smile./Try and be a bit more sympathetic towards her – she's having a hard time at work at the moment.

7 **sympathy** (*for* s.o.)
the ability to be or the feeling of being sympathetic

Have some sympathy for him – he's been very unlucky./I feel absolutely no sympathy for you. It's your own fault you lost your job.

8 **to sympathise** (*with* s.o.)
to feel or express sympathy

I had a similar experience to yours last year, so I sympathise with you.

9 **generous** (*to* s.o.)
happy to give money, kindness, help etc.

They were very generous to us – they gave us a place to stay and never asked us for any money./It's very generous of you to let me borrow your car.

10 **generosity**
the quality of being generous

Thank you for all the generosity you've shown us during our time in England.

11 **to give** (s.o.) **a hand**
to help someone (often in a small way)

Could you give me a hand to carry all these things?

Part 2

1 **to thank** (s.o. *for sth/for doing sth*)
to say thank you

She thanked him for the present./I thanked her for helping me.

Note: **thanks to** = because of

Thanks to her I felt much more confident about my English./We were late, thanks to the traffic.

2 **grateful** (*to* s.o. *for* sth)
wanting to thank someone because
they have been kind to you

I'm very grateful to you for all your help.

3 **gratitude**
the feeling of being grateful

*I wrote to them to express my gratitude for their
hospitality.*

4 **to appreciate** (sth)
to be grateful for something; to
show gratitude for something

*I appreciate your help – it's very kind of you./I'd
appreciate it if you didn't smoke.*

5 **appreciative**
grateful; showing gratitude

*I've gone to all this trouble to get you to the airport on
time. You could at least be a little bit more appreciative.*

6 **appreciation**
the feeling of being appreciative;
gratitude

*This is just a little present to show my appreciation for all
your kindness.*

Part 3

1 **unkind**
not kind; cruel and unpleasant

*That was an unkind thing to say – you know how sensitive
she is.*

2 **inconsiderate**
not considerate; having no thought
for the feelings of others

*Don't you think it's rather inconsiderate to play your
music so loudly at night?*

3 **thoughtless**
inconsiderate

*It was thoughtless of you to go out without telling me
where you'd gone – I was worried.*

4 **unsympathetic**
not sympathetic; not wanting or
unable to sympathise

*When I told him my problem, he was completely
unsympathetic; in fact he hardly even listened.*

5 **selfish**
caring only about yourself and
your wishes; never thinking about
other people

*It was selfish of her to insist that we did what she wanted,
not what we wanted.*

6 **selfishness**
the characteristic of being selfish

*She's had enough of his selfishness – she's going to do
what she wants to do from now on.*

7 **self-centred**
thinking that only you and your
wishes are important

*He's the most self-centred person I've ever met. He never
thinks about his family when he makes a decision.*

8 **mean**
not generous; not wanting to
spend money, give help etc.

*He was so mean that he wouldn't even buy me a drink./
Don't be so mean! Let me have one of your chocolates.*

9 **tight-fisted**
not wanting to spend money; very
ungenerous

He's too tight-fisted to send birthday cards, even to his family.

10 **greedy**
always wanting more (money, food, power etc.)

Don't be so greedy, you've already eaten a lot./She's one of the greediest people I know – never satisfied with what she's got.

11 **greed**
the desire for more

He doesn't need another car – it's pure greed.

Unit 5 Exercises

5.1 *Choose the word or phrase (A, B, C or D) which best completes each sentence.*

1 It was very .... of you to pay for all the drinks last night.
A appreciative   B generous   C grateful   D sympathetic

2 Don't you think it was rather .... of you not to let us know that you weren't coming?
A mean   B unkind   C thoughtless   D unsympathetic

3 You're completely .... ! You never think about anybody but yourself.
A mean   B selfish   C tight-fisted   D greedy

4 It's very .... of you to offer me your seat, but really I'm quite happy to stand.
A sympathetic   B grateful   C considerate   D appreciative

5 She's so .... that she refuses to put the fire on, even in the middle of winter.
A greedy   B selfish   C self-centred   D mean

6 When her father died I wrote her a letter to express my ....
A generosity   B appreciation   C sympathy   D gratitude

7 You've been very .... and I would like to thank you.
A kind   B thoughtless   C grateful   D appreciative

8 It was really .... of her to keep talking when she knew that I was trying to concentrate.
A inconsiderate   B unsympathetic   C helpless   D ungrateful

9 We are very grateful to Professor Humble for his .... in donating this wonderful painting to the museum.
A sympathy   B thought   C generosity   D gratitude

10 My mother was very .... when I failed my exams, in fact she said that it was my own fault for not working harder.
A thoughtless   B unsympathetic   C inconsiderate   D unkind

11 Thank you very much for the card you sent me while I was in hospital. It was very .... of you.
A grateful   B generous   C thoughtful   D appreciative

12 You could at least show your mother some .... for all the things she's done for you.
A kindness   B consideration   C sympathy   D gratitude

5.2 *The word in capitals at the end of each of the following sentences can be used to form a word that fits suitably in the blank space: Fill each blank in this way.*

EXAMPLE We had an interesting *discussion* about football.   DISCUSS

1 The thing I hate most about him is his ....   SELFISH

2 The audience clapped loudly in ....   APPRECIATE

3 It was .... of you to make fun of him like that.   KIND

4 You should try to show a bit more .... for other people,
instead of thinking about yourself all the time.   CONSIDERATE

5 She was very .... when my husband died.   SYMPATHISE

6 There's too much .... in this world.   GREEDY

7 I'll never forget the .... you have shown me.   KIND

8 I did everything I could to make their stay enjoyable, but they
weren't at all ....   APPRECIATE

5.3 *Fill each of the blanks with one suitable word.*

1 Dad, I don't understand my maths homework. Could you .... me a hand?

2 I find it difficult to sympathise .... him.

3 She's so ....-fisted that she'll do almost anything to avoid spending money.

4 Thank you for all your hard work. We're very .... to you.

5 I'd .... it if you could try to be on time tomorrow.

6 We've bought you these flowers to thank you .... your help.

7 It's very sad, but people seem to be becoming more and more ....-centred.

8 You're not going to have another piece of cake are you? That's the fifth you've had, you .... pig!

Unit 6 Polite/Pleasant/Rude/Offensive

Part 1

1 **polite** (*to* s.o.)
having good manners and
consideration for other people;
behaving in a way that is socially
acceptable

*It's polite to let people know if you're going to be late./I
know you don't like my father, but please try to be polite
to him./He gave a polite smile./When you make your
complaint, make sure you're polite about it.*

2 **well-mannered**
(of a person) polite

Their parents brought them up to be well-mannered.

3 **pleasant** (*to* s.o.)
friendly and polite

*He's a very pleasant boy./I'm not particularly keen on her,
but I always try to be pleasant to her.*

4 **nice** (*to* s.o.)
pleasant and friendly

*I met a lot of nice people on holiday./I can't criticise him
because he's always been nice to me.*

5 **to compliment** (s.o. *on* sth)
to say very nice things to
someone about something

Everybody complimented her on her excellent speech.

6 **a compliment**
an expression of admiration or
praise etc.

That was a superb meal. Compliments to the chef!

7 **to pay** (s.o.) **a compliment**
to compliment someone

*He paid her the compliment of saying that she had the
best singing voice he had ever heard.*

8 **to flatter** (s.o.)
to say or suggest that someone is
more attractive or intelligent etc.
than they really are, especially in
order to get something from them

*You're flattering me – I know my German isn't that good./
He flattered her on her new dress, hoping that she might
agree to go out with him that evening.*

9 **flattered**
made to feel pleased and
honoured by something
unexpected happening (indicating
someone's high opinion of you)

*Although I didn't want the job, I was very flattered that
they had offered it to me.*

10 **flattering**
causing you to feel flattered

*Your invitation is very flattering, but I'm afraid I can't
accept.*

11 **flattery**
flattering remarks

Flattery will get you nowhere!

12 **civil**
polite, but often only in the
minimum way, without being
friendly

*Although they don't like each other, they always manage
to be quite civil.*

13 **tactful**
careful not to say or do anything that might offend or upset someone

We decided that it would be tactful to leave, since they obviously wanted to be alone./Hotel receptionists have to be tactful when dealing with difficult customers.

14 **tact**
the ability to be tactful

She showed great tact in her handling of the situation.

15 **diplomatic**
tactful and showing skill in dealing with people

I think that under the circumstances the most diplomatic thing would be to say nothing.

16 **to crawl** (*to* s.o.)
(*colloquial*) to be excessively polite and pleasant to someone, especially someone who is in a superior position to you, because you want some favour from them or because you want them to like you

Nobody likes her at work because she crawls to the boss.

17 **a crawler**
(*colloquial*) a person who crawls

He only got promotion because he's a crawler, not because he deserved it.

Part 2

1 **rude** (*to* s.o.)
not polite (often intentionally)

How old are you, if it's not a rude question?/Didn't anybody teach you that it's rude to stare?/He was rude to me about my work.

2 **bad-mannered/ill-mannered**
(of a person) impolite; having bad manners

Take your feet off the chair and don't be so ill-mannered!/ What bad-mannered young people they are!

3 **cheeky**
lacking respect and politeness (especially for someone that you should respect, for example your parents or teachers); not embarrassed to do or say things that may be considered impolite by others

Do as your father says and don't be so cheeky!/I hope you don't think this is cheeky, but could I help myself to another drink?

4 **cheek**
cheeky behaviour or words

Be quiet! I don't want to hear any more cheek from you./ She's just told me I should get a toupee. What a cheek! (= How cheeky!)

5 **unpleasant** (*to* s.o.)
unfriendly, rude and unkind

Because he's so unpleasant it's difficult to discuss anything with him./Stop being so unpleasant to me. I've done nothing to you.

6 **nasty** (*to* s.o.)
very unpleasant and unkind

That was a nasty thing to say. Why do you dislike her so much?/He's so irritating that it's difficult not to be nasty to him.

7 **hostile**
very unfriendly and aggressive, especially in showing that you do not like someone or something

A rather hostile crowd gathered outside Parliament to protest at the latest cuts in the health service./The village is rather hostile towards tourists.

8 **tactless**
without tact

It was tactless of you to ask about his girlfriend – you know she's left him.

9 **to offend** (s.o.)
to hurt someone's feelings, often unintentionally, by being rude or tactless

I don't know what I've said to offend her, but she's not talking to me./Do you think they'll be offended if I don't go to their party?/He was quite offended that you forgot to send him a birthday card.

10 **offensive**
rude and insulting; causing you to feel offended

His behaviour was so offensive that we left./His offensive remarks about the other guests spoiled the evening.

11 **to take offence** (*at* sth)
to feel offended by something, often unnecessarily

I hope you won't take offence if we ask you to leave now – we're both very tired./She seems to have taken offence at something I said.

12 **to insult** (s.o.)
to deliberately offend someone by being rude to them, usually in what you say

I'll never forgive him for the way he insulted me./I don't mind you saying nasty things about me, but don't insult my mother./I've never been so insulted in all my life!

13 **insulting**
causing you to feel insulted

She made some very insulting comments about his clothes.

14 **an insult**
an insulting remark or action

The argument became very personal, and a lot of insults were exchanged./Their offer is an insult. How do they expect somebody to live on such a miserable salary?

15 **abrupt**
quick and rather rude (especially in wanting to end a conversation)

'I'm far too busy to talk to you now,' he said, in his usual abrupt manner.

16 **short** (*with* s.o.)
abrupt (especially because of anger or impatience)

I didn't mean to be so short with you this morning – it's just that I'm under a lot of pressure at the moment.

17 **crude**
rude, offensive and vulgar

They spent the evening drinking beer and telling crude jokes.

Unit 6 Exercises

6.1 *Choose the word or phrase (A, B, C or D) which best completes each sentence.*

1 He was rather .... me. He just said 'No'.
   A short with   B crude to   C rude with   D tactless to

2 The local people were not very friendly towards us, in fact there was a distinctly ....
   atmosphere.
   A rude   B offensive   C hostile   D abrupt

3 I knew she wasn't going to like what I was going to say, so I tried to find a .... way of
   saying it.
   A civil   B diplomatic   C flattered   D well-mannered

4 Don't you think it's rather .... asking him to lend you more money, when you still haven't
   paid back what you already owe him?
   A cheeky   B hostile   C unpleasant   D crude

5 I'm sorry I was so .... when we met, but I was in a hurry and I couldn't stop and talk.
   A short   B hostile   C abrupt   D unpleasant

6 Don't be so .... ! Where did you learn such bad language?
   A ill-mannered   B crude   C tactless   D nasty

7 It's not very .... to talk with your mouth full.
   A tactful   B gentle   C polite   D educated

8 I find his behaviour towards me quite .... He treats me like an idiot.
   A offending   B insulting   C crude   D ill-mannered

9 I'm .... that you should accuse me of lying.
   A offensive   B insulting   C offending   D insulted

10 Don't be .... ! Say thank you.
   A nasty   B rude   C tactless   D crude

11 I'm sorry about all the .... things I said to you.
   A hostile   B abrupt   C nasty   D short

12 Telling him he was boring wasn't a very .... thing to say.
   A well-mannered   B nice   C flattered   D mannered

13 Why are you always so .... to me? Have I done something to offend you?
   A cheeky   B unpleasant   C tactless   D crude

14 It isn't exactly .... to be told that you're starting to look old.
   A flattering   B well-mannered   C civil   D complimented

15 The interview went very well. Everyone was very .... to me.
   A pleasant   B flattering   C tactful   D diplomatic

16 I dislike him so much that I find it difficult even to be .... to him.
   A tactful   B diplomatic   C civil   D well-mannered

6.2 *The word in capitals at the end of each of the following sentences can be used to form a word that fits
    suitably in the blank space. Fill each blank in this way.*

   EXAMPLE We had an interesting *discussion* about football.   DISCUSS

1 The entire audience took .... at his racist remarks.   OFFEND

34

2 Try to be .... when you tell her the bad news.   TACT

3 I think that with a little .... I could persuade him to change his mind.   FLATTER

4 What a .... , telling him that he's the best teacher she's ever had!   CRAWL

5 What lovely, ... children.   MANNER

6 I find that advertisement .... to women.   OFFEND

7 That was a rather .... remark. You've obviously upset him.   TACT

8 He's the most unpleasant, ... person I've ever met!   MANNER

6.3   *Fill each of the blanks with one suitable word.*

1 That's an .... ! How dare you tell me I'm stupid!

2 You're .... me. I'm not as clever as you say I am.

3 What a .... ! That man just walked straight to the front of the queue.

4 She paid him a .... on his taste in clothes.

5 I'm .... that you have such a high opinion of my work.

6 I hope you won't be .... if I ask you not to smoke.

7 Try to show a bit more .... when you tell your parents you don't agree with them. There's no point in upsetting them by being rude.

Unit 7 Shy/Confident/Arrogant

Part 1

1 **shy**
not confident; nervous in the company of other people

She finds it difficult to talk to strangers because she's shy.

2 **self-conscious**
feeling that everybody is looking at you; nervous because of what they may think

She felt self-conscious because she was the only woman in the room.

3 **inhibited**
self-conscious and unable to act naturally in public

He felt too inhibited to dance./They never enjoy themselves at parties because they're so inhibited.

4 **modest** (*about* sth/*about doing* sth)
not wanting to be admired; not liking to talk about your abilities or qualities

He was very modest about winning and said that he had simply been lucky.

5 **confident**
sure of yourself and your abilities; not nervous even in difficult situations

She's very confident and finds it easy to talk to people she's never met before.

6 **self-confident**
confident; sure of your ability to succeed

I'm sure he'll get the job. He's got such a self-confident manner that he always does really well in interviews.

7 **confidence**
the feeling or characteristic of being confident

You need confidence to make a speech in public.

8 **self-confidence**
the feeling or characteristic of being self-confident

She doesn't have enough self-confidence to try for promotion.

Part 2

1 **arrogant**
behaving as if you are better than everyone else

His arrogant attitude has made him unpopular with the other people in his office./It's arrogant to believe that nobody can do anything better than you can.

2 **big-headed**
thinking that you are a wonderful person, and that you know everything; not modest

Don't get big-headed just because you've passed an exam./People keep telling her she's clever and it's made her big-headed.

3 **vain**
full of love for your own appearance

You're so vain – always looking at yourself in the mirror.

4 **smug**
too satisfied with yourself

If you weren't so smug, you'd realise that the problems I'm talking about might happen to you one day.

5 **cocky**
(*colloquial*) (usually used to talk about men) arrogant; too sure of yourself

He's really cocky – when he walks into a place he acts as if he owns it.

6 **pushy**
always demanding things from other people and trying to get what you want (often rudely)

He's pushy – I've only met him once but he keeps phoning me and asking me to do him favours./He'll never succeed in business – he just isn't pushy enough.

7 **bossy**
fond of giving other people orders (often without being in a position of power)

Don't be so bossy! I'm not your servant.

8 **self-opinionated**
believing that your opinions are always right and refusing to listen to anyone else

He's so self-opinionated that it's impossible to have a reasonable discussion with him.

9 **superior** (*to* s.o.)
believing that you are better than other people

She feels superior to other people because she comes from a wealthy family.

10 **condescending**
behaving as if you are superior to other people; treating other people as if they are inferior or stupid

He's condescending to foreigners because they don't speak the language.

11 **patronising**
condescending

He was really patronising – just because I didn't understand him immediately, he spoke to me as if I was a child.

12 **domineering**
always trying to control other people, without worrying about what they think or feel

She's so domineering – no one else has a chance to say anything when she's there.

13 **to boast** (*about* sth)
to talk too proudly about something that you have got or something that you have done

He's boasting because he passed the exam and nobody else did./He's rich and keeps boasting about how much money he's got, to impress people.

14 **to brag** (*about* sth)
to boast

He's always bragging about his house because it's bigger than anyone else's.

15 **to show off**
to try to impress people and make them admire you

She wore all her expensive jewellery so that she could show off how wealthy she was./Stop showing off! We all know you can speak six languages.

16 **to talk down to** (s.o.)
to talk to someone in a condescending way

I really hate the way she talks down to me all the time – just because she's the boss's daughter

17 **to look down on** (s.o.)
to think that someone is inferior

He looks down on people who don't have as many qualifications as he has.

18 **to be below/beneath** (s.o.)
to be inferior to someone (in their opinion) because of their intelligence, social position etc.

Just because he's been to university he thinks that such a simple job is beneath him./Coming from an upper-class family, she feels that the other students are below her.

Unit 7 Exercises

7.1 *Choose the word or phrase (A, B, C or D) which best completes each sentence.*

1 She's so .... that she doesn't like anyone unless they tell her she's beautiful.
A smug B pushy C self-conscious D vain

2 He's not unfriendly, he's .... Talking to people he's never met before is very difficult for him.
A modest B shy C smug D inferior

3 He was so .... that a lot of the other men in the bar felt like hitting him.
A cocky B self-conscious C proud D boasting

4 He seems to think he's .... me, just because he's been to university.
A superior than B superior to C patronising with D condescending of

5 I can't stand .... people like him. He's always trying to get people to do things for him.
A vain B smug C pushy D patronising

6 Look at the .... way he behaves! Doesn't he think he's great!
A proud B arrogant C self-conscious D pushy

7 'Well, I'll never have to worry about money, unlike some people here,' she said in that ....
voice of hers.
A vain B pushy C bossy D smug

8 Everyone was having fun, but I was too .... to join in, even though I wanted to.
A modest B inhibited C vain D superior

9 He was very .... towards her, saying that she'd done quite well, considering she was a woman.
A smug B cocky C patronising D big-headed

10 He's so .... that he never listens to anyone else's point of view.
A self-opinionated B big-headed C condescending D bossy

7.2 *Fill each of the blanks with one suitable word.*

1 He suddenly felt very .... - .... when he realised that people had noticed the hole in his trousers.

2 I heard him .... to his friends about all the girlfriends he'd had.

3 She's terribly .... at work. She isn't in charge but she keeps telling people what to do.

4 Everyone said he'd been very brave, but he was very .... and said that anyone could have done what he did.·

5 It takes a lot of .... - .... to walk into a room full of strangers and start talking to them.

6 There's no need to .... We all know that you came top of the class in History, you don't have to keep reminding us.

7 She spoke to me in a very .... way, as if I was too stupid to understand such complicated things.

8 He used to be a very modest type of person, but success has made him .... - ....

9 Don't talk .... me! I'm capable of understanding you, I'm not stupid!

10 He's a very .... person and new challenges don't frighten him.

11 She's got a very .... husband who makes it very difficult for her to lead a life of her own.

12 My parents don't want me to marry Steve. Just because he works in a factory, they think he's .... me.

13 She's .... enough to tackle any kind of problem believing that she can solve it.

14 Now that he's rich, he looks .... everyone he knew when he was poor. He doesn't want to see them again.

15 Ever since winning the school tennis competition he hasn't stopped .... it. It seems he wants everyone to know.

16 She doesn't have the .... to do a job that involves selling things to people.

Unit 8 Stubborn/Determined

Part 1

1 **stubborn**
refusing to move, change your mind, co-operate etc.

She's so stubborn that once she's made up her mind, she'll never listen to anything that you say.

2 **obstinate**
stubborn, in spite of attempts to persuade you to do something else

There's no point in arguing with her – she's far too obstinate to listen.

3 **pig-headed**
stubborn and obstinate (often used when people are very angry and want to talk about someone who is stubborn)

For goodness' sake, stop being so pig-headed! It's obvious we've taken the wrong road, so why are you insisting that we haven't?

4 **awkward**
uncooperative; difficult to deal with

I want him to change his plans, but he's being awkward.

5 **to persist** (*with* sth/*in doing* sth)
to continue stubbornly to do something, in spite of opposition or difficulty

If you persist with this kind of behaviour, I shall be forced to sack you./Must you persist in phoning me? I've already told you I don't want to see you./She persisted and eventually mastered the computer.

6 **persistent**
continuing stubbornly to do something, in spite of opposition or difficulty

If he hadn't been so persistent, he wouldn't have got his money back.

7 **persistence**
the action of persisting

It was only after a great deal of persistence that I got a satisfactory answer.

8 **to pester** (s.o.)
to persist in asking or telling someone to do something, in a way that is annoying

The kids have been pestering us to get a video for so long that we've finally agreed to buy one./I really don't like it when people come up to you in the street and pester you for money./Don't pester me now with your complaints!

9 **to be set in your ways**
to have a fixed routine and fixed ideas, which you refuse to change in any way

When people get older, they tend to get set in their ways – eating at the same time every day, and so on.

Part 2

1 **determined** (*to do* sth)
knowing exactly what you want to do and refusing to let anything stop you

She's a very determined woman and I'm sure her business will be a success./I'm determined to finish this, however long it takes.

2 **determination**
the quality of being determined

It takes a lot of determination to succeed in a competitive business.

3 **single-minded**
determined in following only one aim

She's so single-minded about her career that she's never considered marriage or children.

4 **to persevere**
to continue to do something with determination, in spite of difficulties

She persevered and eventually became quite good at playing the violin.

5 **persevering**
continuing to do something with determination, in spite of difficulties

She's a persevering student and should do well.

6 **perseverance**
the quality of persevering

If it hadn't been for the perseverance of one police officer, the murderer would never have been found.

7 **to keep at** (sth)
to persevere with something

I know maths is a difficult subject, but if you keep at it, I'm sure you'll get to understand it.

8 **not to take no for an answer**
to be determined not to allow someone to say no

I've told him that I'm not interested, but he won't take no for an answer.

9 **to stick to** (sth)
to be determined in refusing to change (a decision, promise etc.)

That's my decision and I'm sticking to it.

Unit 8 Exercises

8.1 *Choose the word or phrase (A, B, C or D) which best completes each sentence.*

1 He's .... not to make the same mistakes as before.
A obstinate   B stubborn   C determined   D persevering

2 It's no use trying to persuade him that he's wrong. He's too .... to change his mind.
A stubborn   B persistent   C persevering   D single-minded

3 Learning to drive can be difficult, but I'm sure that if you .... , you'll be able to do it eventually.
A persevere   B keep at   C determine   D stick to

4 Everybody wanted to go to the cinema except Anne, who had to be .... by saying she wanted to go to the theatre.
A single-minded   B persistent   C persevering   D awkward

5 The sales assistant was very .... , and if I didn't like one dress, she would insist on me trying another.
A pig-headed   B persistent   C intent   D single-minded

6 He's been .... her to go out with him for months.
A persisting   B persevering   C pestering   D sticking to

7 She deserves her success because she's been very ....
  A persevering B awkward C pig-headed D set

8 Do as your father tells you, and don't be so .... !
  A set in your ways B obstinate C determined D persevering

8.2 *The word in capitals at the end of each of the following sentences can be used to form a word that fits suitably in the blank space. Fill each blank in this way.*

  EXAMPLE We had an interesting *discussion* about football.   DISCUSS

1 I lost my temper because he was being so .... and was refusing to accept that he was wrong, despite all the evidence.   HEAD

2 I was very impressed by his ....   DETERMINE

3 Her .... was finally rewarded when they agreed they had sent her the wrong bill.
                                                                                PERSIST

4 His success is due to hard work and ....   PERSEVERE

5 She's so .... that she won't let anything stand in the way of her ambition.   MIND

8.3 *Fill each of the blanks with one suitable word.*

1 I told him that I didn't want to go, but he wouldn't .... for an answer.

2 She stuck .... her promise to write to him every day.

3 He persisted .... doing it himself, even though it was quite clear that he wasn't capable of doing it properly.

4 When it comes to the kind of music he likes, he's very .... his ways.

5 Keep .... it! You've nearly finished.

6 The Government is persisting .... its plans to increase taxes, despite opposition.

Unit 9 Tolerant/Intolerant

Part 1

1 **tolerant** (*towards* s.o./*of* sth)
able to accept or allow the opinions, beliefs, behaviour etc. of other people, even though you do not agree (without getting angry)

He's tolerant towards people with different political opinions./She's tolerant of his bad habits.

2 **to tolerate** (sth)
to be tolerant of something; to allow something to happen, even though you do not agree or you find it unpleasant

She tolerates his smoking because she likes him so much./I will not tolerate your rudeness any longer!

3 **tolerance**
the ability to tolerate; the quality of being tolerant

The film is really an appeal for tolerance towards all people, whatever their race or religion.

4 **patient** (*with* s.o.)
able to tolerate unpleasant or difficult situations, or to wait for something, without becoming annoyed

I know he's not the most intelligent pupil in the class, but he does try, so please be patient with him./Be patient – the train will be here soon.

5 **patience**
the quality of being patient

Will you two stop shouting! I'm beginning to lose my patience.

6 **easygoing**
not easily worried or annoyed, and therefore tolerant

He's easygoing – he won't mind if all the plans suddenly change.

7 **broad-minded**
very tolerant of other people's opinions or behaviour, even if they are very different from your own; not easily shocked

I can talk to my parents about absolutely everything. They're very broad-minded.

8 **open-minded**
willing to listen to and consider new ideas, opinions etc.; not judging something before you experience it

Although I'd read a lot of bad things about America, I was quite open-minded when I went there.

9 **to put up with** (s.o./sth)
to tolerate or accept (someone or something annoying or unpleasant) without complaining

I honestly don't know how she puts up with him – he's so selfish!/He puts up with his job because he needs the money.

10 **to stand for** (sth)
(usually used in negative
statements or questions) to accept
or tolerate (something unpleasant)

I'm not going to stand for any more of his insults./Why do you stand for such behaviour?

Part 2

1 **intolerant** (*of* s.o./sth)
not tolerant

She's intolerant of people who don't agree with her./He's intolerant of other people's weaknesses.

2 **intolerance**
the inability or refusal to tolerate

It is intolerance that causes many arguments.

3 **impatient** (*with* s.o.)
not patient

A lot of people say that the British are very impatient with foreigners who don't speak English./Wait your turn and don't be so impatient!

4 **narrow-minded**
having fixed and limited opinions;
unwilling to consider new or
different ideas, opinions etc.

You're so narrow-minded. Can't you accept that someone else might have a point for once?

5 **small-minded**
having an intolerant and
ungenerous mind

How small-minded can you get! Even though they know who I am, the bank insisted that I showed them some identity.

6 **petty**
small-minded, especially in
connection with trivial matters

My boss is so petty, reporting people if they're more than one minute late.

7 **bigoted**
having very strong and often
unreasonable opinions, especially
about politics or religion, and
believing that everyone else is
wrong

He's so bigoted that it's impossible to discuss politics with him.

Unit 9 Exercises

9.1 *Choose the word or phrase (A, B, C or D) which best completes each sentence.*

1 We've got a very .... teacher, who doesn't mind if we're a bit late.
A broad-minded   B open-minded   C easygoing   D tolerated

2 He's very .... , for example he thinks that all unemployed people are lazy and should be made to join the army.
A intolerant   B small-minded   C petty   D bigoted

3 Don't you think you're being rather .... , arguing about such a small sum of money?
A petty   B narrow-minded   C intolerant   D impatient

4 The management is very .... and can't see the long-term benefits of installing a computer.
A petty   B narrow-minded   C intolerant   D small-minded

5 Generally speaking I don't read film reviews because I like to be .... when I go to the cinema.

    A easygoing   B broad-minded   C open-minded   D tolerant

6 The waiter didn't charge you for the extra sugar, did he? How .... can you get?

    A intolerant   B small-minded   C bigoted   D broad-minded

9.2   *The word in capitals at the end of each of the following sentences can be used to form a word that fits suitably in the blank space. Fill each blank in this way.*

    EXAMPLE We had an interesting *discussion* about football.   DISCUSS

1 I'd been standing in the queue for half an hour and was beginning to get rather ....

                                                                                      PATIENT

2 Religious .... forced them to leave the country.   TOLERATE

3 They're very .... people, so the bad language in that film is unlikely to offend them.

                                                                           MIND

4 Hurry up! I'm starting to lose .... with you.   PATIENT

5 They hardly ever argue – I think they're both very .... of each other's faults.

                                                                         TOLERATE

9.3   *Fill each of the blanks with one suitable word.*

1 We're stuck in the traffic, and there's nothing we can do about it, so we'll just have to be ....

2 I don't know how she puts .... his terrible moods; most women wouldn't.

3 That's the third time you've been late this week and I won't .... for it any longer!

4 I don't think she'd be a very good manager as she's so .... of other people's faults.

5 I refuse to .... such insulting behaviour!

6 Unfortunately, the country is not particularly well-known for its racial ....

Section B
Feelings and States of Mind

Units 10-24

Unit 10 Angry/Bad-tempered

1 **angry** (*with* s.o. (*for doing* sth); *about/at* sth)
feeling or showing strong dissatisfaction

There were some angry scenes outside the factory yesterday when the management announced the loss of four hundred jobs./Many people are angry about the Government's decision to increase taxes./She's angry with him for forgetting her birthday.

2 **annoyed** (*with* s.o.; *about/at* sth)
slightly angry, often because of smaller, more ordinary things

I'm really annoyed about missing that train./My mother used to get annoyed with us if we got our clothes dirty.

3 **to annoy** (s.o.)
to cause someone to be annoyed

It annoys me that she never listens to anyone else's opinion.

4 **annoying**
causing you to be annoyed

She's got a really annoying habit of staring at people.

5 **furious** (*with* s.o.; *about/at* sth)
very angry

I'm furious with him for letting me down like that!/He was furious at being made to wait.

6 **to infuriate** (s.o.)
to cause someone to feel furious

The decision to close the village school has infuriated most parents.

7 **infuriating**
extremely annoying

It's infuriating not to be able to get a ticket.

8 **irritated**
annoyed, often because you want something to stop

She seemed rather irritated by his whistling.

9 **to irritate** (s.o.)
to cause someone to feel irritated

His voice irritates me because it's so loud.

10 **irritating**
causing you to feel irritated

It's irritating when people ask stupid questions.

11 **irritable**
tending to get irritated easily and often for no good reason

She's usually quite irritable in the mornings, especially if she's had a late night.

12 **touchy** (*about* sth)
easily annoyed or upset

You're very touchy tonight – I can't seem to say anything right./He's still quite touchy about the break-up of his marriage, so try not to mention it.

13 **bad-tempered**
angry and irritable; tending to get angry easily

He gets bad-tempered when he's tired and shouts a lot.

14 **to have a bad temper**
to get angry frequently and easily

She never argues with him because he's got such a bad temper.

15 **to lose your temper**
to become suddenly and
uncontrollably angry

After being made to wait for over an hour, she finally lost her temper and started screaming at the receptionist.

16 **to go mad/crazy**
(*colloquial*) suddenly to become
very angry

He went mad when I told him that I'd changed my mind./ She'll go crazy if I'm late for dinner.

17 **to have a fit**
(*colloquial*) suddenly to become
very angry

He had a fit when he realised that he would have to do the whole job again.

18 **to take it out on** (s.o.):
to make someone suffer because
you feel angry, even though it is
not their fault

Stop shouting at me! Just because you've had a bad day, it doesn't mean you have to take it out on me.

19 **an outburst**
a sudden explosion of anger

His outburst surprised me – I had no idea he was so angry about the situation.

20 **a tantrum**
a sudden explosion of anger
(especially by a child or by
someone behaving childishly)

He had a tantrum because he couldn't have what he wanted.

21 **frustrated**
dissatisfied or annoyed because
you cannot do what you want to
do or have what you want to have

He's frustrated about not being able to get a job.

22 **to frustrate** (s.o.)
to cause someone to feel
frustrated

It frustrates me that she can't see my point.

23 **frustrating**
causing you to feel frustrated

We've been trying to sell our house for the last year and a half, but without any success. It's so frustrating.

24 **frustration**
the feeling of being frustrated

I can understand your frustration, but it will take some time for you to be able to speak the language well.

25 **to be in a (bad) mood** (*with* s.o.)
to be feeling angry and bad-
tempered

I don't know what I've done wrong but she's obviously in a bad mood with me./Why are you in such a bad mood?

26 **to have had enough** (*of* s.o./sth;
of doing sth)
to be unable to tolerate someone
or something any more; to be fed
up with someone or something

She'd had just about enough of him, so she told him to leave./We've had enough of your insults./I've had enough of listening to other people's problems – it's beginning to annoy me.

27 **to be sick of/tired of/sick and tired of** (s.o./sth/doing sth)
to be completely fed up with someone or something

I'm sick of other people taking advantage of me./Do you ever get tired of all the things that are written about you by the press?/I'm sick and tired of hearing your complaints.

28 **to get on someone's nerves**
to irritate and annoy someone

The noise outside is getting on my nerves.

29 **to get up someone's nose**
(*colloquial*) to irritate someone very much

Politicians get up my nose – they'll say one thing one minute, and something else the next.

30 **to make you sick**
to make you very angry

It makes me sick that some people get rich by cheating others.

31 **a nuisance**
an annoying person or thing; someone or something that causes you problems

James is being a real nuisance at the moment – he keeps phoning me up in the middle of the night, saying he's got to talk to me./It's a nuisance having to wait, but we haven't got much choice.

32 **a pain in the neck**
(*colloquial*) an irritating person or thing; a big nuisance

It's a pain in the neck having to do this. I'd much rather be watching television.

33 **the final/last straw**
the final event in a series of annoying events which causes you to get angry

After a six-hour delay at the airport, it was the final straw when they boarded the plane only to find there was no food for their journey.

Unit 10 Exercises

10.1 *Choose the word or phrase (A, B, C or D) which best completes each sentence.*

1 Everyone was surprised by his .... because nobody had ever seen him get angry before.
  A explosion   B outburst   C outpouring   D frustration

2 He's very childish. Every time something happens that he doesn't like he has a ....
  A bad temper   B frustration   C tantrum   D bad mood

3 I've never seen anyone so .... ! I thought he was going to hit me.
  A touchy   B sick   C irritable   D angry

4 The transport strike is a real .... because it will make it very difficult for me to get to work.
  A pain in the back   B nuisance   C last straw   D frustration

5 It's not my fault the car has broken down, so don't take it .... me.
  A from   B to   C out of   D out on

6 I'm .... in my present job; I need something more challenging.
  A irritated   B annoyed   C frustrated   D crazy

7 That's the last .... ! I'm leaving.
  A pain   B straw   C limit   D nuisance

8 She's a(n) .... old woman, who's always complaining about something.
  A annoyed   B furious   C bad-tempered   D infuriated

9 He's very .... about his work, so try not to say anything that he might take as a criticism.
  A annoyed   B touchy   C irritated   D annoying

10 My boss will be absolutely .... with me for being late again.
  A angry   B annoyed   C furious   D irritated

11 My father has a very bad ....
  A temper   B mood   C humour   D tantrum

10.2 *The word in capitals at the end of each of the following sentences can be used to form a word that fits suitably in the blank space. Fill each blank in this way.*

  EXAMPLE We had an interesting *discussion* about football.   DISCUSS

1 It's .... not being able to speak a foreign language.   FRUSTRATE

2 Most people tend to be rather .... when they're tired.   IRRITATE

3 It's .... having to wait so long for an answer.   ANNOY

4 There's nothing worse than the .... of being stuck in a traffic jam
  when you're in a hurry to get somewhere.   FRUSTRATE

5 He's got some very .... habits.   IRRITATE

6 It's .... when people won't believe things that are obviously true.   FURIOUS

10.3 *For each of the sentences below, write a new sentence as similar as possible in meaning to the original sentence, but using the word given. This word must not be altered in any way.*

  EXAMPLE   It's no use arguing: I've made up my mind.
            point

  ANSWER   *There's no point in arguing; I've made up my mind.*

1 She'll be furious when she finds out what's happened.
  go

  ....

2 He got angry because we all disagreed with him.
  temper

  ....

3 She is angry and bad-tempered today.
  mood

  ....

4 I don't want to be treated as an inferior any more!
  sick

  ....

5 He got extremely angry when he saw the damage that had been done to his car.
  fit

  ....

6 His arrogance irritates me.
nose

  ....

7 I don't want people to order me about any more.
enough

  ....

8 Waiting for buses irritates me.
nerves

  ....

9 Having to get up so early is irritating.
neck

  ....

10 It annoys me to see so much food being wasted.
sick

  ....

Unit 11 Certain/Optimistic/Doubtful/Pessimistic

1 **certain** (*of*/*about* sth; *that* ...)
having no doubt in your mind
about something

He's not certain what her name is./I'm certain (that) she doesn't like me./She doesn't like me – I'm certain of it.

2 **sure** (*of*/*about* sth; *that* ...)
certain

Are you sure (that) he said he was coming?/It was him who caused the accident, I'm sure of it./Have you got a map? I'm not quite sure about the way.

3 **to make certain/sure**
　a (*of* sth/*that* ...)
　to check in order to be certain

He looked all around to make certain that nobody was listening./I think this is your train but you'd better ask the guard to make sure (of it).

　b (*of* sth/*of doing* sth/*that* ...)
　to do something in order to be
　certain of something else

England scored twice in the last ten minutes to make certain of victory./We left early to make sure of getting there on time./Make sure (that) you're not late.

4 **positive** (*of*/*about* sth; *that* ...)
completely sure

'Are you sure you locked the door?' – 'Yes, I'm positive.'/She was positive (that) she had met him before somewhere./Are you positive of/about what happened?

5 **confident** (*of* sth/*of doing* sth/
that ...)
certain that something will happen
as you want it to happen

She was confident (that) she would win./We're confident of victory./He's confident of finishing the job on time.

6 **hopeful** (*of* sth/*of doing* sth/
that ...)
fairly confident

I'm hopeful (that) everything will turn out well in the end./She's not very hopeful of success./Although the concert is sold out, he's hopeful of getting a ticket at the door.

7 **hopefully**
let us hope (that ...)

Hopefully, I'll be feeling better tomorrow./See you next week, hopefully.

8 **optimistic** (*about* sth/*that* ...)
always expecting the best; hopeful
about the future

We're optimistic that our money problems will soon be over./She's optimistic about her chances of getting the job.

9 **an optimist**
a person who is always optimistic

You must be a real optimist if you think that the bank are going to agree to lend you all that money.

10 **to hope for the best**
to be hopeful that things will go
well (especially when there is
reason to believe that they will
not)

Her attitude towards exams is to do a bit of revision the night before, and just hope for the best!

11 **to look on the bright side**
to find something to be hopeful
about in spite of problems

'I've just lost my job and my wife is asking for a divorce.' – 'Look on the bright side – at least you've still got your friends.'

Part 2

1 **doubtful** (*about* sth)
uncertain and unconfident

I'm doubtful (about) whether she'll come./I've agreed to lend him my car, but I still feel a bit doubtful about it.

2 **to doubt**
   a (s.o./sth)
to be uncertain about someone or something

I'm sorry if I doubted you – you proved me wrong./She apologised for having doubted my word (= for having thought that I was not telling the truth.)

   b (*that* ...)
to consider something to be unlikely

She may be there tonight, but I very much doubt it./I doubt that she'll be there./I doubt whether they'll come.

3 **doubt** (*about* sth)
(a feeling of) uncertainty

There seems to be some doubt about whether he is actually guilty or not./There's no doubt that she's lying./ Everyone thinks it's a wonderful idea, but I have my doubts./Now that I'm finally leaving the country forever, I'm beginning to have doubts about it.

4 **no doubt**
certainly or very probably (used to emphasise that you believe something to be true)

No doubt you'll have heard about their engagement./We'll see you tonight, no doubt.

5 **sceptical** (*of*/*about* sth)
very doubtful about something; unwilling to believe that a claim, statement, promise etc. is true

I've assured her that my offer is genuine, but she still seems rather sceptical (of/about it).

6 **pessimistic** (*about* sth)
always expecting the worst

He's very pessimistic about his chances of passing his exams.

7 **a pessimist**
a pessimistic person

Don't be such a pessimist! You've got as good a chance as anybody of getting the job.

8 **a reservation** (*about* s.o./sth)
a feeling of doubt about someone or something, that causes you to hesitate

She's beginning to have reservations about marrying him./ My biggest reservation about buying it, is the price./We accept your offer without reservation.

Unit 11 Exercises

11.1 *Choose the word or phrase (A, B, C or D) which best completes each sentence.*

1 Are you .... that those were his exact words?
  A positive B hopeful C secure D safe

2 He seems .... about whether she'll agree or not.
  A doubtful B undoubted C unlikely D without doubt

3 She's .... that she'll get the job. She thinks she did well in the interview.
A confident   B doubtless   C trustworthy   D safe

4 I'm .... it. I saw it happen with my own eyes.
A confident for   B sure from   C certain of   D positive from

5 He says he might come, but he ....
A doubts   B doubts it   C doubts so   D doubts about it

11.2 *Fill each of the blanks with one suitable word.*

1 I couldn't remember if I'd closed all the windows, so I went back to make ....

2 I always think that things will turn out well. I guess you could call me an ....

3 She's confident .... getting into university.

4 You're such a .... ! You always think that something is going to go wrong.

5 The manufacturers are claiming that it is a miracle drug, but many doctors and scientists still have their .... about it.

11.3 *For each of the sentences below, write a new sentence as similar as possible in meaning to the original sentence, but using the word given. This word must not be altered in any way.*

EXAMPLE   It's no use arguing: I've made up my mind.
point

ANSWER   *There's no point in arguing; I've made up my mind.*

1 I'm hoping to go skiing at Christmas.
hopefully

2 I don't think his reasons for being nice to me are sincere.
sceptical

3 Think about the good things! You're young and healthy and will have plenty more opportunities.
bright

4 Do you think that your chances of getting promotion are good?
optimistic

5 I don't quite understand the meaning of this word.
sure

6 All I can do is cross my fingers and be optimistic.
best

7 I expect he'll be late, as usual.
   doubt

   ....

8 I can only see bad things happening in the future.
   pessimistic

   ....

9 I wasn't sure about him at first, but now he seems very good at his job.
   reservations

   ....

10 Does she think that her chances of getting the job are good?
   hopeful

   ....

Unit 12 Confused/Bewildered

1 **confused**
 a (*about* sth)
 (of a person) unable to understand something (often because it does not seem to be logical); uncertain or unclear

 I'm afraid I'm rather confused – could you explain from the beginning again?/I'm confused about what to do./A lot of people get confused by rules and regulations.

 b (of something, a situation etc) difficult to understand; not clear

 The plans are rather confused at the moment so I don't know what's going to happen.

2 **to confuse**
 a (s.o.)
 to make it difficult for someone to understand or think logically.

 Do you have to use all those technical terms? They just confuse me.

 b (a situation etc.)
 to make it difficult to understand

 You've already changed your plans twice – if you change them again you'll just confuse things even more.

 c (s.o./sth *with* s.o./sth else)
 to think, by mistake, that one thing is another

 I think you're confusing me with someone else – I've never met you before in my life./I always confuse them because they look so alike.

3 **confusing**
 causing you to be confused

 The road signs were so confusing that I didn't know which way to go.

4 **confusion**
 the feeling of being confused; a situation where everything is confused

 Her explanation only added to his confusion./There was a lot of confusion because nobody knew where to go.

5 **to cause confusion**

 The changes in the law have caused a lot of confusion.

6 **puzzled**
 unable to understand or explain something, often because it seems strange or unusual

 The doctor was clearly puzzled by my illness./I'm puzzled about why she decided to leave./I'm puzzled that someone as intelligent as yourself should want to leave university after only one year.

7 **to puzzle** (s.o.)
 to cause someone to be puzzled

 His attitude puzzles me.

8 **puzzling**
 causing you to be puzzled

 His failure in the exam is puzzling, since he's one of the better students.

9 **baffled**
 completely unable to explain or understand something, or find a solution to it; very confused

 I was baffled by the question./Police are baffled as to who could have committed such a crime.

10 **to baffle** (s.o.)
 to cause someone to be baffled

 His decision to leave the company baffles me.

11 **baffling**
causing you to be baffled

It's a baffling situation and I really can't explain it.

12 **mixed-up**
confused (perhaps for emotional
or social reasons)

*A lot of young people are mixed-up about their futures./I'm
getting mixed-up now – are you talking about Richard or
his brother?/He's been so mixed-up since his wife left him.*

13 **to mix up** (s.o./sth *with* s.o./sth
else)
to confuse two things, so that you
think that one thing is the other

*I mixed her up with someone else because I've got a bad
memory./Aunt Sheila is always mixing up the twins and
calling them by their wrong names./I always mix those
two words up and use one when I should use the other.*

14 **a mix-up**
a confused arrangement

*It was a mix-up – I thought we were meeting at 8 o'clock
but he thought we were meeting at 7 o'clock.*

15 **bewildered**
completely confused and unable to
understand something

*Don't ask me to explain the film to you – I'm as
bewildered as you are./I'm bewildered as to why she's so
angry – she was perfectly friendly this morning.*

16 **to bewilder** (s.o.)
to cause someone to be
bewildered

*Even after ten years, his behaviour still bewilders me at
times.*

17 **bewildering**
very confusing and difficult to
understand (often because many
new and different things are
happening at the same time)

*Her first visit to India was an exciting but bewildering
experience.*

18 **lost**
confused; unable to follow (an
explanation, argument etc.)

*I'm lost – could you explain that all again, please?/I don't
know what's happening in this film – I'm totally lost.*

19 **mystified**
very puzzled; unable to even
begin to understand something
because it is so strange

*Don't ask me why it happened – I'm as mystified as you
are./She was mystified by Dr Jackson's comment – what
could he have meant?*

20 **to mystify** (s.o.)
to cause someone to be mystified

The rules of the game completely mystify me.

21 **mystifying**
causing you to be mystified

*Most foreigners find the game of cricket completely
mystifying.*

22 **mysterious**
unable to be explained or
understood; strange and causing
you to wonder

*It's very mysterious – she suddenly disappeared but
nobody knows where she went.*

23 **a mystery** (*to* s.o.)
something strange that cannot be
explained or understood

I have no idea why that happened – it's a mystery to me.

24 **not to be clear** (*about* sth)
to be confused; not to understand

If there's anything you're not clear about, please ask./I'm not clear (about) what you want me to do – could you explain it again?

25 **to be unable to think straight**
to be unable to think clearly
because of confusion, pressure,
panic etc.

He asked me so many questions that I couldn't think straight.

Unit 12 Exercises

12.1 *Choose the word or phrase (A, B, C or D) which best completes each sentence.*

1 My first day at work was .... because there were so many new things to take in.
   A confused   B puzzling   C bewildering   D mystifying

2 Statistics .... – all those numbers!
   A baffles me   B mixes me up   C mixes me   D loses me

3 You're talking too fast – I'm getting .... !
   A lost   B puzzled   C mystified   D baffled

4 Considering his unhappy childhood, it's not surprising he's so ....
   A mystified   B lost   C baffled   D mixed-up

5 Due to an administrative .... , the room had been double-booked.
   A confusion   B mix-up   C puzzle   D mystery

6 She's usually very calm, so I must admit I'm rather .... as to why she lost her temper like that.
   A confusing   B puzzled   C mixed-up   D bewildering

12.2 *The word in capitals at the end of each of the following sentences can be used to form a word that fits suitably in the blank space. Fill each blank in this way.*

    EXAMPLE We had an interesting *discussion* about football. DISCUSS

1 He's behaving in a very .... way. MYSTERY

2 There seems to be some .... about what she actually said. CONFUSE

3 Her sudden disappearance is rather .... PUZZLE

4 I'm .... as to how such a thing could have happened. BEWILDER

5 The instructions are very .... I can't tell what I'm supposed to do. CONFUSE

6 The police were .... – why should anyone want to steal a wastepaper basket? MYSTIFY

12.3 *For each of the sentences below, write a new sentence as similar as possible in meaning to the original sentence, but using the word given. This word must not be altered in any way.*

EXAMPLE   It's no use arguing: I've made up my mind.
           point
ANSWER   *There's no point in arguing; I've made up my mind.*

1 If you change all the plans now, you'll only confuse things.
   confusion

   ....

2 I find the whole subject very confusing.
   bewilders

   ....

3 What I don't understand is why he did such a strange thing.
   puzzles

   ....

4 I'm not sure what you want me to do.
   confused

   ....

5 They look so alike that it's very easy to confuse her with her sister.
   mix

   ....

6 I was so worried that my mind couldn't function normally.
   straight

   ....

7 We can't explain his disappearance.
   mystery

   ....

8 You're not the first person to mistakenly think that I am my twin brother.
   confuse

   ....

9 I don't understand how to fill in this form.
   clear

   ....

Unit 13 Vague/Incomprehensible/Clear _____

Part 1

1 **vague**
not certain or definite (of
something said or written); not
clear (of a feeling, idea, memory
etc.)

He's rather vague about his plans – I don't think he knows what he's going to do./I've got a vague feeling that something is wrong.

2 **faint**
not strong or clear (of a feeling,
colour, sound etc.)

I have a faint memory of being here before./The photographs are a bit faint./(On the phone) 'You're very faint. I can hardly hear you.'

3 **ambiguous**
able to be understood in more
than one way, and therefore
unclear or confusing

His answer was ambiguous – I'm not sure if he agreed or not.

4 **muddled**
confused and disorganised

The arrangements are muddled, so I don't know where or when we're meeting./I'm getting muddled – what do I have to do now?

5 **garbled**
not clear; confused (of an
explanation or statement)

His explanation was so garbled that I have no idea what actually happened.

6 **inarticulate**
unable to express yourself clearly;
not clearly expressed (of speech)

He had drunk so much that he was completely inarticulate./He woke up suddenly, made a few inarticulate noises, then fell asleep again.

7 **unintelligible**
impossible to understand (perhaps
because something is garbled or
not clearly expressed)

His accent is so strong that he's unintelligible.

8 **incomprehensible**
impossible to understand

This document is incomprehensible.

9 **illegible**
impossible to read (because the
writing is unclear)

His handwriting is illegible.

10 **inexplicable**
impossible to explain

I find your behaviour quite inexplicable.

Part 2

1 **clear** (*to s.o.*)
easy to understand and without
confusion

When you arrive, you'll be given clear instructions about what to do./What's the problem? It all seems perfectly clear to me.

2 **to be clear** (*about* sth)
to understand something
completely

I asked her to explain again because I wanted to be clear about what I had to do./I wasn't clear whether she was talking to me or not.

3 **clearly**
without doubt

This is clearly a matter for the courts to decide./When I asked him he didn't answer. He clearly didn't understand what I was saying.

4 **to clear** (sth) **up**
to find a solution to, or remove
doubt about something (a
problem, misunderstanding etc.)

I've called this meeting to try to clear up any misunderstandings.

5 **to make** (sth) **clear**
to explain something (your
feelings or intentions etc.) in a
way that is easy to understand

I had a word with him because I wanted to make my feelings clear – he understands now./I would like to make it clear that I'm not criticising you.

6 **to clarify** (sth)
to make something clearer and
easier to understand (especially by
giving more information or
explaining more simply)

We've asked the management to clarify exactly what its intentions are./Could you clarify this point for me – does this train leave every day except Sunday, or only on Sunday?

7 **obvious**
clear; easy to see or understand

He was terribly rude – it's obvious that he planned to offend me./Her reason for lying is obvious – she was too embarrassed to tell me the truth.

8 **obviously**
clearly

She had a terrible time. Obviously she won't go there again./She obviously hates me./He's obviously having a bad time.

9 **to sink in**
to become clear in the mind; to
become completely understood
(often of sudden or surprising
events)

Things happened so fast that it took a long time for them to sink in./Winning a gold medal hasn't really sunk in yet.

10 **to take** (sth) **in**
to understand and absorb
something completely

Everything happened so quickly that I couldn't take it all in./I don't think I took in anything of what he said.

11 **to make** (sth) **out**
to see, hear, read, understand etc.
clearly

The road sign is too far away – I can't make out what it says./I couldn't make out what he was saying – there was too much noise./Can you make out the signature on this letter?/I can't make out why she left – I thought she was happy here.

Unit 13 Exercises

13.1 *Choose the word or phrase (A, B, C or D) which best completes each sentence.*

1 We left New York when I was six, so my recollections of it are rather ....
   A faint   B muddled   C garbled   D unintelligible

2 His papers were so .... that he couldn't find what he was looking for.
   A garbled   B ambiguous   C muddled   D inarticulate

3 He speaks so quickly that most of the things he says are ....
   A inexplicable   B unintelligible   C illegible   D inarticulate

4 I've got a(n) .... idea what you mean.
   A ambiguous   B faint   C muddled   D vague

5 She was so angry that she became quite ....
   A vague   B garbled   C inarticulate   D inexplicable

6 I asked him what to do but his instructions were so .... that I still didn't understand.
   A inexplicable   B garbled   C muddled   D illegible

7 Her sudden disappearance was ....
   A unintelligible   B illegible   C inarticulate   D inexplicable

8 Her comment was so .... that some people thought she was pleased while others thought she was annoyed.
   A incomprehensible   B ambiguous   C unintelligible   D faint

9 The report was written in technical language, which would have been .... to most people.
   A incomprehensible   B illegible   C inarticulate   D garbled

10 The signature at the bottom of the page was totally ....
   A inarticulate   B ambiguous   C incomprehensible   D illegible

11 Could you .... that last remark?
   A clear   B clarify   C clear out   D make clear

12 He .... that nothing would change his mind.
   A cleared   B cleared up   C made clear   D made it clear

13.2 *For each of the sentences below, write a new sentence as similar as possible in meaning to the original sentence, but using the word given. This word must not be altered in any way.*

EXAMPLE   It's no use arguing: I've made up my mind.
          point

ANSWER   *There's no point in arguing; I've made up my mind.*
          ....

1 The news of his death was such a shock that it hasn't been fully understood yet.
sunk

....

2 There are a few problems which we ought to try to find a solution to.
clear

....

3 She clearly doesn't like me.
obvious

....

4 He's got such a strong accent that half the time I can't understand a word he's saying.
   make

   ....

5 He gave us so much information that it was impossible to absorb everything.
   take

   ....

6 It's obvious that he doesn't understand you.
   obviously

   ....

7 Do you understand how to find my house?
   clear

   ....

Unit 14 Embarrassed/Ashamed

1 **embarrassed** (*about* sth/*about doing* sth)
uncomfortable, often because you feel stupid (and perhaps causing you to become red in the face)

He's embarrassed about losing his hair./I was too embarrassed to tell her how much I liked her.

2 **to embarrass** (s.o.)
to cause someone to feel embarrassed

It embarrasses her when people ask her personal questions./Stop it! Can't you see you're embarrassing him?

3 **embarrassing**
causing you to feel embarrassed

I got to work this morning and found I had put on different coloured socks – it was so embarrassing!

4 **embarrassment**
the feeling of being embarrassed

I hope I haven't caused you any embarrassment.

5 **an embarrassment** (*to* s.o.)
an embarrassing person or thing

His past mistakes are an embarrassment to him./She's an embarrassment to her family.

6 **humiliated**
made to feel small or stupid

I was so humiliated that I just wanted to get out of there as quickly as possible.

7 **to humiliate** (s.o.)
to embarrass someone very much, by making them feel stupid

She humiliated him by shouting at him in front of all his friends.

8 **humiliating**
causing you to feel humiliated

The England team suffered a humiliating 12-0 defeat.

9 **humiliation**
the feeling of being humiliated

The bridegroom waited and waited, but the bride didn't arrive. Can you imagine the humiliation?

10 **ashamed** (*of* s.o./sth)
feeling embarrassment or guilt because of your own or someone else's wrong or inappropriate behaviour

He's ashamed of the way he behaved last night – he ruined the evening./He's ashamed of himself for behaving so badly./I'm ashamed of her for saying such things.

11 **shame**
the feeling of being ashamed

He said that he looked on the terrible things he'd done with shame./The memory of that evening filled him with shame.

12 **to feel guilty** (*about* sth/*about doing* sth)
to feel that you have done something wrong

She felt guilty about lying to him for days afterwards.

13 **guilt**
the feeling of being guilty

She must have stolen it – you can see the guilt all over her face.

14 **to have a (guilty) conscience**
(*about* sth/*about doing* sth)
to feel guilty, often for a long
period of time

He's got a (guilty) conscience about stealing when he was young.

15 **to feel responsible** (*for* sth)
to feel that something is your fault

I feel responsible for the argument, because what I said started it.

16 **to feel a fool**
to feel embarrassed or humiliated

I felt such a fool when I realised that he'd been lying to me all the time.

17 **to make a fool of** (s.o.)
to humiliate someone or make
them feel or look stupid

She made a fool of him by telling everyone his embarrassing secret.

18 **to go red/to blush**
to become red in the face because
of embarrassment or shame

He went red after he told a joke and nobody laughed./She blushed when she realised she'd said something stupid.

19 **to be reduced to** (sth/*doing* sth)
to be forced into a humiliating
position, inferior to your previous
situation

He used to be the boss, but now he's reduced to working for someone else./After losing his job, he was reduced to sweeping the streets for a living.

Unit 14 Exercises

14.1 *The word in capitals at the end of each of the following sentences can be used to form a word that fits suitably in the blank space. Fill each blank in this way.*

EXAMPLE We had an interesting *discussion* about football. DISCUSS

1 I'll never forget the .... I felt in that situation. HUMILIATE

2 I've never been so .... in all my life! EMBARRASS

3 He feels a great deal of .... for the awful way he behaved. ASHAMED

4 His face went bright red with .... EMBARRASS

5 I was .... by the way he made everyone laugh at me. HUMILIATE

6 I think I walked into the room at an .... moment for them. EMBARRASS

7 It's .... to be laughed at in public. HUMILIATE

8 She was tormented by feelings of .... GUILTY

14.2 *Fill each of the blanks with one suitable word.*

1 I feel guilty .... leaving you to do all the work.

2 I'm ashamed .... what I said. Can you forgive me?

3 It was wrong of him to .... a fool of her in public like that.

4 He .... because he was embarrassed – his face went bright red.

5 She's embarrassed .... not being able to speak the language well.

14.3 *For each of the sentences below, write a new sentence as similar as possible in meaning to the original sentence, but using the word given. This word must not be altered in any way.*

    EXAMPLE   It's no use arguing: I've made up my mind.
                point
    ANSWER   *There's no point in arguing; I've made up my mind.*

1 Things have got so bad that I have to borrow money from other people.
reduced

2 I felt stupid when I realised what I'd done.
fool

3 Her lack of education makes her feel embarrassed.
embarrassment

4 She blushed at the mention of his name.
red

5 He thinks that the accident was his fault.
responsible

6 He feels bad about cheating them.
conscience

7 She feels uncomfortable when people tell her how beautiful she is.
embarrasses

8 The boss likes to make people feel embarrassed in front of others.
humiliate

Unit 15 Frightened/Terrified

1 **fear** (*of* sth)
the horrible feeling that you have
when you think that danger is
near, or that something terrible
may happen

*My greatest fear is that one day I'll be old and helpless./
The child was shaking with fear./Claustrophobia is a fear
of confined places.*

2 **afraid**
   a (*of* s.o./sth; *that* ...)
   experiencing fear or worry

*She was so afraid that she was shaking./You haven't seen
Jackie, have you? I'm afraid that something awful might
have happened./I'm afraid of dogs./I'm just going to give
you a little injection – it's nothing to be afraid of.*

   b (*of* doing sth)
   experiencing fear because of
   something bad that may happen

I'm afraid of being robbed.

   c (*to do* sth)
   not wanting to do something
   because of fear

*I was afraid to walk home alone, so I got a taxi./If there's
anything you don't understand, don't be afraid to
interrupt.*

3 **frightened**
afraid

*I ran away because I was frightened./He's frightened that
he'll never fully recover from the accident./Many children
are frightened of the dark./I'm frightened of losing my
job./I was frightened to argue in case he hit me.*

4 **to frighten** (s.o.)
to cause someone to feel
frightened

His threats frightened me.

5 **frightening**
causing you to feel frightened

I used to find being on my own at night really frightening.

6 **a fright**
a moment of fear; a frightening
experience

The noise gave me a fright.

7 **scared**
frightened or worried

*I didn't say anything because I was scared./They were
scared that someone would hear them./He's scared of his
father./He's scared of failing./She's too scared to
complain.*

8 **to scare** (s.o.)
to cause someone to feel scared

His temper scares her.

9 **scary**
frightening

Did you see the late film last night? Scary, wasn't it?

10 **a scare**
a frightening experience

*What are you doing standing there in the dark like that?
You gave me quite a scare./It was only a mild heart
attack, but enough to give him a scare.*

11 **terrified**
extremely frightened

It was an awful flight – I was terrified./He spent the next two weeks moving from one place to another, terrified that someone would recognise him./He's terrified of heights./I was terrified of having an accident./I was terrified to tell him the truth.

12 **to terrify** (s.o.)
to cause someone to feel terrified

The thought of dying terrifies me.

13 **terrifying**
causing you to feel terrified

It was a terrifying journey because he's such a bad driver.

14 **terror**
enormous fear

He watched in terror as the man pulled out a gun.

15 **petrified**
terrified; so frightened that you can hardly move

They're petrified to go out because they live in such a violent area./She held her bag tightly, petrified that someone would try to steal it.

16 **to petrify** (s.o.)
to cause someone to feel petrified

Those big police dogs petrify me.

17 **petrifying**
causing you to feel petrified

Being on my own in a strange country was petrifying at first.

18 **to fear** (s.o./sth; *that ...*)
to be afraid of someone or something; to worry that something (unpleasant) may happen or have already happened

He didn't take the risk because he feared the consequences./I fear (that) I'll never see him again./I haven't had the exam results yet but I fear the worst.

19 **for fear of** (*doing* sth)
because of not wanting something (unpleasant) to happen

I said nothing for fear of starting an argument.

20 **to dread** (sth/*doing* sth)
to fear greatly; to be very afraid of something that is going to happen or may happen

I dread these weekly visits from the doctor./She dreads getting his letters in case they're bad news./I'm dreading the interview tomorrow.

21 **I dread to think**
I hate to imagine

I dread to think what he'll say when I tell him what really happened.

22 **not to dare** ((*to*) *do* sth)
not to have the courage to do something; to be too afraid to do something

I wouldn't dare (to) argue with my boss – he'd fire me./I daren't ask her for any more money./We were all so frightened of her that we didn't dare (to) complain.

23 **not to have the nerve** (*to do* sth) not to have the courage to do something

I wouldn't have the nerve to argue with him./I haven't got the nerve to ask him./Nobody had the nerve to tell her she was wrong.

Unit 15 Exercises

15.1 *Choose the word or phrase (A, B, C or D) which best completes each sentence.*

1 The thought of another world war is a .... prospect.
A scaring   B dreading   C frightened   D terrifying

2 The documentary gave him such a .... that he gave up smoking immediately.
A terror   B fear   C fright   D dread

3 He didn't really mean it. He only said it to .... you.
A dread   B frighten   C fear   D afraid

4 I'm not going to visit him because I have a .... of hospitals.
A fright   B scare   C fear   D dare

5 I wouldn't .... talk to people in such a rude way in case they hit me.
A nerve   B dare   C dread   D fear

6 He didn't react to the film at all but it .... me.
A terrorised   B dreaded   C terrified   D feared

7 He didn't tell anyone because he was .... that nobody would believe him.
A feared   B dared   C afraid   D frightening

8 The thought of being trapped in a fire .... me.
A terrors   B fears   C petrifies   D dreads

9 The smell of hospitals fills her with ....
A terror   B afraid   C scare   D petrify

10 I .... being attacked. I hope it never happens.
A scare   B daren't   C dread   D petrify

11 I was absolutely .... It took me ages to stop shaking.
A dreaded   B petrified   C feared   D scary

12 It was a(n) .... moment. I thought something terrible was going to happen.
A afraid   B scaring   C scary   D dreading

13 The car gave me .... I thought it was going to hit me.
A a scare   B a terror   C a fear   D scare

14 The look on his face when he attacked me was absolutely .... ! I'll never forget it.
A scaring   B petrifying   C fearing   D afraid

15 I'm .... Don't leave me alone in this awful place.
A scared   B dreading   C fearing   D dreadful

16 I'm .... that something terrible's going to happen if I'm not very careful.
A scary   B frightened   C dreaded   D feared

17 He was .... that someone would find out he'd been stealing.
A terrific   B dreaded   C dreadful   D terrified

15.2 *For each of the sentences below, write a new sentence as similar as possible in meaning to the original sentence, but using the word given. This word must not be altered in any way.*

EXAMPLE   It's no use arguing: I've made up my mind.
point

ANSWER   *There's no point in arguing; I've made up my mind.*
....

1 I didn't have the courage to tell him what I really thought.
dare

....

2 Some people don't go out because of the amount of crime.
frightened

....

3 He frightens me.
afraid

....

4 I said nothing because I thought that I might offend her.
fear

....

5 They have three locks on the door because they don't want to be burgled.
afraid

....

6 The prospect of making that speech at the wedding tomorrow terrifies me.
dreading

....

7 I agreed with him because I didn't want to make the situation even worse.
scared

....

8 I don't know what's going to happen but I'm very pessimistic.
worst

....

9 I'm being very careful because I don't want to make a mistake.
frightened

....

10 The thought frightens me.
frightening

....

11 I don't want to imagine how much it's going to cost.
dread

....

12 When I think what the world might be like in twenty years' time I feel frightened.
scares

....

13 I wouldn't dare say a thing like that.
nerve

....

14 Guns terrify me.
terrified

....

Unit 16 Happy/Willing

1 **happy**
   a (*about* sth/*that* ...)
   feeling good (especially because something good has happened or because life in general is good)

   She's such a happy child./I hope you'll both be very happy together./He's happy about getting the job he wanted./I'm so happy that you've changed your mind about leaving.

   b giving pleasure

   Those were the happiest days of my life./Their marriage has always been very happy.

   c (*about* a situation/*with* sth)
   satisfied that something is good or right

   She's not very happy about the time it's taking him to finish the job./I'm happy with the progress you're making.

   d (*for* s.o.)
   happy because someone else is happy

   Congratulations on getting your new job. I'm so happy for you.

2 **happiness**
   the feeling of being happy

   At last she has found happiness.

3 **pleased**
   happy or satisfied (especially because of something good that has happened)

   I expect you'll be pleased to get back to work again after so long, won't you?/What are you looking so pleased about?/I'm really pleased you could come./Are you pleased with your new car?/He's been promoted and I'm pleased for him.

4 **to please** (s.o.)
   to cause someone to feel pleased

   It pleases me to see her so happy./He's a difficult man to please.

5 **pleasing**
   causing you to feel pleased

   It's quite pleasing to be finally proved right.

6 **pleasure**
   the feeling of being pleased

   I get a lot of pleasure from music.

7 **a pleasure**
   an enjoyable experience

   It's been a pleasure talking to you.

8 **glad**
   pleased and happy

   I'm glad you phoned. I've been trying to ring you all morning./I'm glad to hear that you've changed your mind about leaving.

9 **satisfied** (*with* sth)
   happy because you have what you want or need, or because something is good enough for you

   I don't want to change my job – I'm satisfied with the one I've got.

10 **to satisfy** (s.o.)
   to cause someone to feel satisfied

   You're always complaining. Nothing ever seems to satisfy you.

11 **satisfying**
causing you to feel satisfied

What you need is a satisfying meal./Getting my first book published was a very satisfying experience.

12 **satisfactory**
good enough for a particular purpose; acceptable

He didn't give me a satisfactory explanation.

13 **satisfaction**
the feeling of being satisfied

She gets a lot of satisfaction from her job.

14 **excited** (*about* sth)
full of energy and happiness (because of something that is happening or going to happen)

I'm excited about going on holiday tomorrow.

15 **exciting**
causing you to feel excited

It was a really exciting match./I find London a really exciting city.

16 **excitement**
the state of being excited

The discovery has caused great excitement amongst scientists./Life is so boring at the moment – I need some excitement.

17 **delighted**
very pleased or excited

I'm delighted with my new flat./Thank you for the invitation – we'd be delighted to come.

18 **delightful**
very pleasant; lovely

That was a delightful meal, thank you.

19 **thrilled**
extremely pleased and excited

I'm thrilled for you. Congratulations!/She's thrilled about meeting the Queen next week.

20 **thrilling**
very exciting

It was a thrilling game of football – one of the most exciting I've ever seen.

21 **a thrill**
a strong feeling of excitement; a very exciting experience

She gets a real thrill out of parachuting./Meeting the Prime Minister was an enormous thrill.

22 **cheerful**
happy and lively

He's always cheerful – nothing gets him down.

23 **to cheer** (s.o.) **up**
to stop (someone) being unhappy

Cheer up! Things aren't that bad./I was feeling awful, so your phone call really cheered me up.

24 **to enjoy** (sth/*doing* sth)
to get pleasure from something

I enjoy good food./I enjoy meeting new people.

25 **to enjoy yourself**
to be happy because of what you are doing

He didn't want to leave the party because he was enjoying himself so much.

| 26 | **enjoyable** | *It was a good party – I had a very enjoyable evening.* |

26 **enjoyable**
giving pleasure

It was a good party – I had.a very enjoyable evening.

27 **enjoyment**
the feeling of enjoying something

The bad weather spoiled our enjoyment of the holiday.

28 **to have a good time**
to enjoy yourself

I had a good time while I was in England.

29 **to look forward to** (sth/*doing* sth)
to feel happy or excited about a future event

I'm really looking forward to the concert./We're both looking forward to going on holiday next month.

30 **to be willing** (*to do* sth)
not to mind doing something; to be ready or prepared to do something

I'm willing to work hard because I want to do the job well./He wasn't willing to wait so he left.

31 **willingness**
the state of being willing

His willingness to work hard was noticed by the boss.

32 **to be happy/pleased/glad to do sth**
to be very willing to do something

I'll be happy to give you any help you might need./I was glad to be of some assistance./Our representative will be pleased to answer any enquiries you may have.

33 **to be prepared to do sth**
to be willing to do something

I'm not in a hurry – I'm prepared to wait.

Unit 16 Exercises

16.1 *Choose the word or phrase (A, B, C or D) which best completes each sentence.*

1 The children were .... with the toys you sent. In fact they haven't stopped playing with them!
A satisfied   B excited   C thrilled   D glad

2 She won't be .... until she gets what she wants.
A satisfied   B excited   C thrilled   D glad

3 He was clearly .... to see her again.
A delightful   B delighted   C cheerful   D cheered

4 Are you .... you came? Have you had a good time?
A cheerful   B glad   C excited   D cheered

5 I don't know what was wrong with her tonight. She's usually quite ....
A pleased   B glad   C cheerful   D satisfied

6 My first time in an aeroplane was a real .... for me.
A happiness   B satisfaction   C excitement   D thrill

16.2 *The word in capitals at the end of each of the following sentences can be used to form a word that fits suitably in the blank space. Fill each blank in this way.*

EXAMPLE We had an interesting _discussion_ about football.   DISCUSS

1 Thank you for a very .... evening.   ENJOY

2 If your work is .... , you will get a longer contract.   SATISFY

3 He showed great .... to compromise.   WILLING

4 It was a .... experience which I shall never forget.   THRILL

5 She gets a lot of .... from reading.   ENJOY

6 What a .... place!   DELIGHT

7 Seeing her play performed for the first time gave her a great sense of ....   SATISFY

8 It's quite an .... film because you don't know what's going to happen until the end.   EXCITE

9 Are you going to Germany on business or for .... ?   PLEASE

10 I'm bored. I need some .... in my life.   EXCITE

11 Money does not always bring ....   HAPPY

16.3 *Fill each of the blanks with one suitable word.*

1 I don't want a bigger house. I'm happy .... the one I've got.

2 I've just heard about your engagement. I'm really happy .... you.

3 Are you excited .... leaving?

4 She's very pleased .... getting the job. It's exactly what she wanted.

5 Congratulations! I'm very pleased .... you.

16.4 *For each of the sentences below, write a new sentence as similar as possible in meaning to the original sentence, but using the word given. This word must not be altered in any way.*

EXAMPLE   It's no use arguing: I've made up my mind.
           point

ANSWER   *There's no point in arguing; I've made up my mind.*

1 I hope you have a good time.
enjoy

....

2 I bought myself a present because I wanted to stop myself feeling unhappy.
cheer

....

3 I don't mind discussing it with you.
willing

....

76

4 Did you enjoy yourself last night?
   time

   ....

5 I don't mind doing whatever you want me to do.
   happy

   ....

6 It was good to see all my old friends again.
   enjoyed

   ....

7 I don't mind working hard, if that's what I have to do.
   prepared

   ....

8 Do you like your new car?
   pleased

   ....

9 She won't like me changing the arrangements.
   happy

   ....

10 I'm very excited about seeing you next week.
    looking

    ....

Unit 17 Unhappy/Reluctant

1 **unhappy** (*about* sth)
not happy or satisfied

Cheer up! What have you got to look so unhappy about?/ She left because she was unhappy about the way she'd been treated.

2 **unhappiness**
the state of being unhappy

After years of unhappiness, she's finally found something she enjoys doing.

3 **sad**
a not happy; causing you to feel unhappy

I'll be sad to leave because I've made a lot of good friends here./The film has got a very sad ending./I'm afraid I've got some sad news for you.

b very unfortunate

I think it's sad that some people are forced to sleep on the streets.

4 **sadness**
the feeling of being sad

I left with a feeling of sadness.

5 **miserable**
very unhappy

I've had a miserable day today – nothing has gone right.

6 **misery**
the state or feeling of being very unhappy

His face was a picture of misery.

7 **depressed**
very unhappy and without hope (often over a long period of time)

She's been rather depressed recently – I think she's got family problems.

8 **to depress** (s.o.)
to cause someone to feel depressed

That programme about the famine in Africa really depressed me.

9 **depressing**
causing someone to feel depressed

I hate winter – it's such a depressing time of year.

10 **depression**
the state of being depressed; extreme unhappiness

She suffers from depression.

11 **fed up** (*about* sth)
unhappy and perhaps dissatisfied

I'm fed up – it's been a terrible day and I just want to forget it./What are you looking so fed up about?

12 **to get** (s.o.) **down**
to make someone unhappy

This terrible weather really gets me down.

13 **upset** (*about* sth)
unhappy, worried or emotionally troubled (because something unpleasant has happened to you personally)

She got upset when her boss told her that her work was no good./I'm upset about losing my diary because it had the phone numbers of all my friends in it.

14 **upsetting**
causing someone to be upset

It's very upsetting to be accused of stealing.

15 **to upset** (s.o.)
to cause someone to feel upset

It upset him when she said he looked stupid in his new suit.

16 **hurt**
in a state of emotional pain or unhappiness (because someone who you like has said or done something unpleasant to you)

I'm not angry, I'm just hurt that you didn't feel you could trust me.

17 **hurtful**
unkind; causing someone to feel hurt

I know I said a lot of hurtful things to you last night and I just want you to know that I'm sorry.

18 **to hurt** (s.o.)
to cause someone to feel hurt

It hurt her parents when she said she never wanted to see them again.

19 **disappointed** (*about*/*at* a situation; *in*/*with* s.o./sth)
unhappy because what was expected did not happen or was not as good as you had hoped for

She's very disappointed at not getting in to university./He was disappointed about his failure to get promotion./I'm disappointed in him – I thought he was honest./They were disappointed with the hotel, which had looked better in the brochure.

20 **to disappoint** (s.o.)
to cause someone to feel disappointed

His answer disappointed me. I had expected something better.

21 **disappointing**
causing you to feel disappointed

It was a disappointing holiday. It rained all the time.

22 **a disappointment**
a disappointing person or thing

The film was a huge disappointment./I've been a disappointment to my parents./Life is full of disappointments.

23 **disillusioned** (*with* s.o./sth)
unhappy and disappointed as a result of learning that someone or something that you believed in is not as good as you thought

He left his job because he was disillusioned with the whole profession.

24 **moved**
made to feel sadness or sympathy; emotionally affected

They were moved by the pictures they saw of people dying of starvation.

25 **touched**
emotionally affected (especially because someone has been kind to you)

I was touched when they bought me a present because I wasn't expecting one.

26 **lonely**
unhappy because you have no friends

It's very easy to get lonely if you live in a big city.

27 **to miss** (s.o./sth)
to be unhappy because someone or something is not with you

She's in a foreign country and she misses her home and her family.

28 **reluctant** (*to do* sth)
unwilling to do something and therefore slow to do it

I was reluctant to leave because I was having a good time.

29 **reluctance**
the feeling of not wanting to do something; slowness to act because of being reluctant

He finally apologised but with a great deal of reluctance.

30 **to complain** (*to* s.o. *about* sth/ *that* ...)
to say that you are unhappy or dissatisfied with something

She's always complaining because nothing's ever good enough for her./I complained to the manager about the service./He complained that his meal was not properly cooked.

31 **a complaint**
a statement of why you are unhappy or dissatisfied; a reason to complain

We've received several complaints about your behaviour./ I've got no complaints about the way I was treated.

32 **to make a complaint**
to complain formally

I phoned the manager to make a complaint.

33 **to moan**
to complain continually (especially without having a very good reason)

You're always moaning about something. If it's not your job, it's your flat. If it's not your flat, it's your car. If it's not your car, it's something else.

Unit 17 Exercises

17.1 *Choose the word or phrase (A, B, C or D) which best completes each sentence.*

1 It's very .... that they've got so many problems, but I don't know what I can do about it.
   A miserable   B disappointing   C sad   D unhappy

2 He's been rather .... since his wife died.
   A alone   B lone   C lonely   D solo

3 I was very .... to receive your lovely letter.
   A reluctant   B upset   C emotional   D touched

4 We had to listen to him .... about how he didn't have any money.
   A crying   B mumbling   C groaning   D moaning

5 I'm not angry so much as .... I don't expect friends to deceive me and you have done.
   A moved   B touched   C hurt   D depressed

6 A lot of people seem .... the present government.
   A disappointed about   B disillusioned with   C depressed by   D deceived by

7 The film was very powerful and we were all .... by it; in fact it made most of us cry!
   A touched   B moved   C upset   D fed up

17.2 *Fill each of the blanks with one suitable word.*

1 I wonder what he's so unhappy ....

2 I'm disappointed .... you. I thought I could rely on you but obviously I can't.

3 He's always complaining .... something.

4 I'm fed .... about not having any money.

5 Are you disappointed .... losing?

17.3 *The word in capitals at the end of each of the following sentences can be used to form a word that fits suitably in the blank space. Fill each blank in this way.*

EXAMPLE We had an interesting *discussion* about football.   DISCUSS

1 That was a very .... thing to say.   HURT

2 It was a very .... experience and it took a long time to get over it.   UPSET

3 That's one of the most .... stories I've ever heard.   DEPRESS

4 There's enough .... in the world without people making films about it. SAD

5 Has the doctor given you anything for your ....?   DEPRESS

6 It was with a certain amount of .... that he left.   RELUCTANT

7 The food was rather ....   DISAPPOINT

8 He's caused his parents a lot of ....   UNHAPPY

9 I didn't go out last night because I was .... and I didn't want to see anyone.
                                                                                              DEPRESS

10 You're always .... Isn't there anything that makes you happy?   MISERY

17.4 *For each of the sentences below, write a new sentence as similar as possible in meaning to the original sentence but using the word given. This word must not be altered in any way.*

EXAMPLE   It's no use arguing: I've made up my mind.
point

ANSWER   *There's no point in arguing; I've made up my mind.*

1 If you want to express your dissatisfaction, you'll have to see the manager.
complaint

....

2 I don't want to criticise him because he's a good friend of mine.
reluctant

....

3 When I was away, I wished that my family were with me.
missed

....

4 Her job is making her miserable.
down

....

5 We were expecting her to win, so we were upset when she didn't.
disappointment

....

Unit 18 Interested/Enthusiastic/Bored

Part 1

1 **interested** (*in* sth/*in doing* sth)
having or showing a desire to
know or learn more about
something, to give your attention
to it or to do it

*Don't tell me about your problems – I'm not interested./
She's always been quite interested in music./We're thinking
of going to the theatre tomorrow night. Are you interested
in coming?*

Note: **interested** + infinitive =
interested by what you learn or
discover. Verbs frequently used in
this construction include *to see*, *to
hear*, *to find out*, *to know*, *to read*
etc.

I'm interested in reading. (= I'm interested in the activity
of reading.)
I was interested to read your letter. (= I was interested by
what I read.)

2 **to interest** (s.o.)
to cause someone to be interested

*Football doesn't interest me./It may interest you to know
that the film you were talking about is on TV next week.*

3 **interesting**
causing you to be interested

*She's very interesting – I could listen to her for hours./It's
an interesting book./That's an interesting question.*

4 **interest** (*in* sth)
the state or feeling of being
interested

*He didn't show much interest in what I was saying./The
play was too long – we were all beginning to lose interest
by the end./Anyone with an interest in the future of our
planet should read this book./Your problems are of no
interest to me.*

5 **an interest**
something that you give your time
and attention to, and that you
enjoy doing or learning about

*His only interest at the moment seems to be watching
television./We get on well because we share the same
interests.*

6 **enthusiastic** (*about* sth)
very interested, excited and
positive about something, in such
a way that it shows in how you
talk and behave

*'Are we going to Richard's party tonight?' – 'I suppose
so' – 'Well, you don't sound very enthusiastic. Don't you
want to go?'/She's enthusiastic about her new job.*

7 **enthusiasm** (*for* sth)
the state or feeling of being
enthusiastic

*Her speech was received with enthusiasm by the crowd./
She didn't show much enthusiasm for any of my
suggestions.*

8 **fascinated**
extremely interested; unable to
take your attention away from
something

*Go on, finish your story: I'm fascinated – what happened
next?/Having never been to a foreign country before, she
was fascinated by everything she saw.*

9 **to fascinate** (s.o.)
to cause someone to be fascinated

*I've been to the exhibition several times because some of
the paintings fascinate me./She fascinates me – I wonder
what she's really like.*

10 **fascinating**
causing you to be fascinated

Rome is a fascinating city./It's been fascinating talking to you./He's had a fascinating life – you should hear some of his stories.

11 **fascination**
the state or feeling of being fascinated

The children watched in fascination as the egg cracked open and a tiny creature emerged./Your little boy seems to have a fascination with that box – he's been playing with it for hours.

12 **obsessed** (*with/by* s.o./sth)
able only to think about one thing, and nothing else; interested in an unhealthy way

He's completely obsessed by her./She's obsessed with the thought of death.

13 **an obsession**
something with which you are obsessed

For many people, football isn't simply an interest – it is an obsession.

14 **fanatical** (*about* sth)
excessively enthusiastic about something in a way that is considered to be unreasonable

Her boss is fanatical about punctuality./Wherever he went, Elvis Presley was greeted by fanatical crowds.

15 **a fanatic**
a person who is fanatical about something

He's a fitness fanatic and is always doing some kind of sport.

16 **to be into** (sth)
(*colloquial*) to be very interested in something

She's really into politics./I'm not so keen on going to the cinema these days. I'm more into the theatre.

Part 2

1 **bored** (*with* sth/*with doing* sth)
dissatisfied because you have nothing to do; not interested and therefore not wanting to continue with something

I'm bored. Let's go out, shall we?/She soon got bored with her new toys./I'm bored with talking about this – can't we change the subject?

2 **to bore** (s.o.)
to cause someone to be bored

To tell you the truth, politics bores me./I hope I'm not boring you, am I?

3 **boring**
causing you to be bored

What an incredibly boring evening that was!/He's a rather boring speaker, isn't he?/I live a pretty boring life – nothing exciting ever happens to me.

4 **boredom**
the state of being bored

The worst thing about the job is the boredom.

5 **a bore**

  a a person who bores other people, especially by talking too much about something in an uninteresting way

  She's such a bore – all she ever talks about is work.

  b something that is boring or annoying

  The meeting was a bore – it seemed to go on for ages./I find shopping a real bore.

6 **to bore** (s.o.) **stiff/to death/to tears**

  to bore someone very much

  I was bored stiff by the conversation./She bores me to death when she starts talking about all her children./The film bored me to tears.

7 **fed up** (*with* sth/*with doing* sth)

  bored with something, especially something that you have had too much of or that has been continuing for too long

  I'm fed up with this book – nothing's happened in the last thirty pages./I got fed up with waiting for him, so I left.

8 **dull**

  boring and unexciting

  He's one of the dullest people I've ever met – his conversation can send you to sleep!/I come from a rather dull town where nothing much ever happens.

Unit 18 Exercises

18.1 *Choose the word or phrase (A, B, C or D) which best completes each sentence.*

1 He's .... his health, and takes dozens of vitamins every day.
  A obsessed in B fascinated by C fanatical about D enthusiastic about

2 I'm not really .... this kind of music. I prefer music you can dance to.
  A in B for C into D with

3 She's .... with the idea that somebody is following her. I think she ought to see a psychiatrist.
  A enthusiastic B fascinated C obsessed D fanatical

4 It was a very .... evening. Nothing really happened.
  A dull B fed up C disinterested D bored

5 Many young children have a(n) .... with fire.
  A interest B obsession C fascination D enthusiasm

6 He's a really .... person. He talks all the time but he never says anything interesting.
  A bored B boring C fed up D annoyed

18.2 *The word in capitals at the end of each of the following sentences can be used to form a word that fits suitably in the blank space. Fill each blank in this way.*

  EXAMPLE We had an interesting *discussion* about football.   DISCUSS

1 I thought it was a fantastic idea at first but I've lost some of my .... now.
                                                  ENTHUSIASTIC

2 It was a .... place and I'd like to have been able to stay longer.   FASCINATE

3 The thing I hate most about being unemployed is the ....   BORING

4 I wish you'd show some .... in this matter, because it's important.   INTERESTING

5 It's worrying to think what might happen if such weapons fell into the hands of ....
                                                                                    FANATICAL

6 Tennis started as a hobby for him but it's become an .... now.   OBSESSED

7 The whole evening was a .... and I couldn't wait to leave.   BORING

8 Her .... include swimming and reading.   INTERESTING

18.3 *For each of the sentences below, write a new sentence as similar as possible in meaning to the*
      original sentence, but using the word given. This word must not be altered in any way.

   EXAMPLE   It's no use arguing: I've made up my mind.
             point

   ANSWER   *There's no point in arguing; I've made up my mind.*

1 I found the stories she told me very interesting.
  fascinated

   ....

2 He sounded as if he was really looking forward to staying with us for the weekend.
  enthusiastic

   ....

3 Making money interests him more than anything else.
  interested

   ....

4 I've lost interest in this programme; let's watch something else.
  bored

   ....

5 It would interest me to know why it happened.
  interested

   ....

6 She gets bored with things very quickly.
  bore

   ....

7 Is there anything in that magazine that you're interested in?
  interests

   ....

8 I find grammar exercises extremely boring.
  stiff

   ....

9 I've lost interest in going to the same places all the time.
  fed up

   ....

Unit 19 Jealous/Resentful

1 **jealous**
   a (*of* s.o./sth)
   unhappy and angry because
   someone has what you want;
   wanting to have what someone
   else has

   If he's rude to you, it's only because he's jealous./She's always been rather jealous of her older sister./Everybody's jealous of his success.

   b unhappy and angry because
   you think that someone is being
   too intimate with someone who
   you feel belongs to you

   He gets incredibly jealous if he sees his wife talking to other men.

2 **jealousy**
   the feeling of being jealous

   The motive for the murder seems to have been jealousy.

3 **envious** (*of* s.o./sth)
   wishing that you could have what
   someone else has or that you
   could be like them

   I'm envious of their lifestyle. If only I could afford to live like that./He's envious of his brother.

4 **to envy** (s.o./sth)
   to feel envious of someone or
   something

   I really envy her. I wish I had so many friends./I envy his determination./I don't envy you the long drive home. (= I'm glad I don't have to do it.)

5 **envy**
   the feeling of being envious

   He looked at his friend's brand new car with obvious envy.

6 **bitter** (*about* sth)
   angry because you feel that you
   have been badly treated

   He's still bitter about the way he was forced to leave his job.

7 **bitterness**
   the feeling of being bitter

   She still talks about him with bitterness. I don't think she'll ever forgive him for what he did to her.

8 **resentful**
   angry or bitter about something
   that you think is unfair

   She's resentful about the way she's been treated at work.

9 **to resent** (sth/*doing* sth)
   to be angry or bitter about
   something that you think is unfair

   She resents his interference./I resent having to work when everyone else is on holiday.

10 **resentment**
   the feeling of being resentful

   The offer of a five per cent pay increase, when the management are getting ten per cent, has caused a great deal of resentment amongst the work force.

11 **to have a chip on your shoulder**
to feel bitter or resentful because
you feel that you are inferior or
that you have been treated
unfairly

*He's got a chip on his shoulder about not being as
intelligent as his brother.*

12 **spiteful**
wanting to hurt or annoy someone
who has hurt you or who you do
not like

*I'm sure she only said she didn't like my new hairstyle to
be spiteful./That's a spiteful thing to say!*

13 **to spite** (s.o.)
(usually only used in the
infinitive) to hurt or annoy
someone deliberately

The child carried on shouting to spite his parents.

14 **to have/bear a grudge** (*against*
s.o.)
to continue to feel bitter towards
someone who has hurt you in the
past

*She has/bears a grudge against the company and will
never forgive them for the way they treated her.*

15 **to begrudge** (s.o. sth)
to feel that someone does not
deserve what they have got, and
feel resentful about it

*I begrudge him his promotion – I'm the one who should
have got it, not him./I don't begrudge her her high salary
– she works hard.*

16 **a grievance**
something that you feel is unfair
and that you have reason to
complain about

*Her main grievance is that she isn't treated as an equal at
work.*

17 **revenge**
a (*on* s.o.)
something that is done in order to
hurt someone who has hurt you
(and which gives you satisfaction)

*The terrorist attack was an act of revenge./He took revenge
on all his former enemies.*

b (in sport) victory following a
defeat

*It's always disappointing to lose, but we'll get our revenge
in next year's final.*

18 **to get your own back** (*on* s.o.)
to get revenge on someone

*One day I'll get my own back on them for the terrible way
they treated me.*

19 **to retaliate**
to do something bad to someone
in return for them having done
something bad to you

He hit me, so I retaliated and hit him back.

Unit 19 Exercises _____

19.1 *Choose the word or phrase (A, B, C or D) which best completes each sentence.*

1 She's still very bitter .... what happened.
   A about   B with   C of   D for

2 He put salt in her coffee to .... her.
   A revenge   B begrudge   C retaliate   D spite

3 Any employee who has a complaint or .... should take the matter to his or her manager.
   A resentment   B bitterness   C grievance   D revenge

4 He slapped me and I .... by kicking him.
   A revenged myself   B avenged   C retaliated   D resented

5 She gets .... if her husband goes out with other women.
   A envious   B resentful   C jealous   D bitter

6 I bear no .... against him, despite what he did to me.
   A resentment   B bitterness   C grievance   D grudge

7 He swore that he would get his .... on the men who had hurt him.
   A spite   B revenge   C retaliation   D resentment

19.2 *The word in capitals at the end of each of the following sentences can be used to form a word that fits suitably in the blank space. Fill each blank in this way.*

EXAMPLE We had an interesting *discussion* about football.   DISCUSS

1 I have always .... your lifestyle.   ENVIOUS

2 .... can be a dangerous emotion.   JEALOUS

3 The teacher tends to have favourites which causes a lot of ....
  amongst the other pupils.   RESENT

4 Children can be very ....   SPITE

5 The incident left him with feelings of anger and ....   BITTER

6 I was green with .... when I saw her new house.   ENVIOUS

19.3 *For each of the sentences below, write a new sentence as similar as possible in meaning to the original sentence, but using the word given. This word must not be altered in any way.*

EXAMPLE   It's no use arguing: I've made up my mind.
          point

ANSWER   *There's no point in arguing; I've made up my mind.*
          ....

1 She's angry that she is treated like the office slave.
  resents

  ....

2 He feels bitter and inferior because he didn't go to university.
  chip

  ....

3 He got revenge on her.
   own

   ....

4 They resent not getting paid what they think they should be paid.
   resentful

   ....

5 I don't feel resentful towards her – she deserves her success.
   begrudge

   ....

6 I envy their happy relationship.
   envious

   ....

Unit 20 Sorry

1 **to be sorry**
 a (*about* sth/*to do* sth/*that* ...)
 to feel regret or unhappiness
 about something

 I'm sorry about last night – it was my fault./I was sorry to hear about your problems. Can I help?/I'm sorry (that) I'm late./I'm sorry (that) you didn't enjoy the film./I'm sorry if I offended you – I didn't mean to be rude.

 b (*for* sth/*for doing* sth)
 to regret something bad that you
 have done

 I'm sorry for what I said./I'm sorry for shouting at you – I was feeling tired.

 c (*to do* sth)
 to regret having to do something,
 because the other person will not
 like it

 I'm sorry to say this but I think you're talking rubbish./ I'm sorry to tell you that you've failed your exam.

2 **to be/feel sorry for** (s.o.)
 to feel sympathy or pity for
 someone

 I'm sorry for him – he's got a lot of problems./I feel sorry for her, being married to a man like him.

3 **to apologise** (*for* sth/*for doing* sth)
 to say that you are sorry

 She apologised for her behaviour./He apologised for keeping me waiting.

4 **an apology**
 a statement that you are sorry

 I owe you an apology – I was rude to you./I've accepted his apology and so the subject is closed.

5 **an excuse**
 a reason, often false for why you
 have or have not done something,
 or why you cannot do something

 That's the third time you've been late this week – what's your excuse this time?

6 **to make an excuse**

 I didn't want to talk to him so I made an excuse. I said I was busy.

7 **I'm afraid** (*that* ...)
 I am sorry to have to tell you
 (that ...)

 I'm afraid (that) I won't be able to come tonight./'Could I speak to Mr Richards?' – 'He's out at the moment, I'm afraid. Can I take a message?'/'Have you seen my watch anywhere?' – 'I'm afraid not.'

8 **to regret** (*that* ...)
 (*formal*) to be sorry

 I regret that I will be unable to attend your wedding.

Unit 20 Exercises

20.1 *Fill each of the blanks with one suitable word.*

1 I .... sorry .... her. She's had a terrible life.

2 He said he was sorry .... the mistake and that it would never happen again.

3 I didn't want to go out with them so I .... an .... and told them I had to work late.

4 Your behaviour was disgraceful. We demand an immediate ....

5 There's no need to .... It wasn't your fault.

6 I'm terribly sorry .... causing you so much trouble.

20.2 *For each of the sentences below, write a new sentence as similar as possible in meaning to the original sentence, but using the word given. This word must not be altered in any way.*

    EXAMPLE   It's no use arguing: I've made up my mind.
                    point
    ANSWER   *There's no point in arguing; I've made up my mind.*

1 I'm sorry, but I'm rather busy at the moment.
afraid

    ....

2 He said that he was sorry he hadn't told me before.
apologised

    ....

3 I didn't like leaving that house because I liked living there.
sorry

    ....

4 We won't be able to come to your party and we're sorry.
regret

    ....

5 I feel bad about having to inform you that we no longer need you.
sorry

    ....

Unit 21 Surprised/Shocked

1 **surprised** (*at* s.o. (*for doing* sth); *at/by* sth; *that* ...)
experiencing or showing surprise

She had a surprised look on her face./We were all surprised to hear that you're leaving./I'm not surprised that she left him./She seemed surprised by his reaction./ I'm surprised at you for saying such things.

2 **to surprise** (s.o.)
to cause someone to feel surprised

So many strange things have happened recently that nothing surprises me any more.

3 **surprising**
causing you to feel surprised

It was a surprising thing for him to say, considering how polite he usually is.

4 **surprise**
the feeling caused by something unexpected or unusual happening

Imagine my surprise when she told me that she was not only pregnant, but expecting twins!

5 **a surprise**
an unexpected or surprising event

The present was a complete surprise.

6 **to come as a surprise** (*to* s.o.)
to cause someone to be surprised

His bank statement came as a surprise to him because he thought he had more money in his account./It comes as no surprise to me that she failed, considering that she didn't do any work.

7 **astonished** (*at/by* sth; *that* ...)
very surprised about something

She was astonished at the lack of security at the airport./ I'm astonished that you don't know the name of our Prime Minister.

8 **to astonish** (s.o.)
to cause someone to feel astonished

It astonishes me that she made such a bad decision.

9 **astonishing**
causing you to feel astonished

It's astonishing that such an unfair system can be allowed to exist.

10 **amazed** (*at* s.o. (*for doing* sth); *at/by* sth; *that* ...)
so surprised about something that you find it difficult to believe

We were all amazed to learn how old he was./I'm really quite amazed that you haven't heard of him./I'm amazed at how much things have changed recently./I'm amazed at her for making such a stupid mistake.

11 **to amaze** (s.o.)
to cause someone to feel amazed

You amaze me!/It always amazes me how young she looks for her age.

12 **amazing**
causing you to feel amazed

What amazing news!/I find her ignorance amazing.

13 **incredible**
very surprising and difficult to believe

Have you heard the news – isn't it incredible?

14 **shocked** (*at*/*by* sth)
unpleasantly surprised, upset or
offended

A shocked silence followed the announcement of the President's death./She was shocked when he told her that he wanted a divorce./My father's not easily shocked, but even he thought the film was obscene.

15 **to shock** (s.o.)
to cause someone to be shocked

It shocked him to see how ill she had become./The programme shocked many viewers with its violence and bad language.

16 **shock**
the strong emotional disturbance
caused when something unpleasant
happens

She wasn't injured in the accident, but she was suffering from shock.

17 **a shock**
an unpleasant surprise

It came as a complete shock to me when they told me I'd lost my job.

18 **staggered** (*at*/*by* sth)
extremely surprised and shocked
because something is hard to
believe (often the size, amount or
extent of something)

The whole country was staggered by the suggestion of a scandal within the Royal Family./I was staggered at the prices in that shop.

19 **staggering**
causing you to feel staggered

The mistake is calculated to have cost the company a staggering £47,000,000./I find it absolutely staggering that so many people are out of work in such a prosperous country.

20 **shattered**
shocked and extremely upset
because of a personal tragedy

He was shattered by the death of his father – they were very close.

21 **shattering**
causing you to feel shattered

The news that the factory was to close clearly had a shattering effect on her.

22 **stunned**
so shocked or surprised by
something (pleasant or unpleasant)
that you are unable to speak or
react

She was stunned to hear that she had won the competition./He was completely stunned by their accusations.

23 **speechless**
unable to speak because of
surprise, shock or anger

She was so delighted by the diamond ring he had bought her that she was speechless./His rudeness left her speechless.

24 **startled**
surprised and often slightly
frightened by a sudden noise or
movement

She had a startled look on her face./I was startled when the dog started barking.

25 **to startle** (s.o.)
to cause someone to be startled

She startled him by creeping up behind him and touching him on the shoulder.

26 **to make** (s.o.) **jump**
to startle someone

The bit in the film where the hand suddenly comes crashing through the window really made me jump.

27 **to take** (s.o.) **by surprise**
to surprise someone by happening unexpectedly

I wasn't expecting her until eight o'clock, so it took me by surprise when, at half past six, the doorbell rang./The rain took us entirely by surprise.

28 **to catch** (s.o.) **off guard**
to surprise someone by doing something when they are not expecting it

My question about her boyfriend seemed to catch her off guard./I was caught off guard by their arrival, as I'd only just got up.

29 **to catch** (s.o.) **unawares**
to catch someone off guard

I was caught unawares by your phonecall and didn't know what to say./Am I too early? I hope I haven't caught you unawares.

30 **to take** (s.o.) **aback**
to surprise or shock someone in such a way that for a moment they are unable to say anything

I was rather taken aback when my five-year-old niece asked me where babies came from!/Her angry outburst took me aback.

31 **out of the blue**
suddenly and unexpectedly

'Were you expecting promotion' – 'No, it came right out of the blue.'/She arrived out of the blue./They offered me the job completely out of the blue.

32 **no wonder**
an expression meaning that something is not surprising in view of the circumstances

'I told him I thought he was an idiot.' – 'No wonder he doesn't talk to you anymore!'

Unit 21 Exercises

21.1 *Choose the word or phrase (A, B, C or D) which best completes each sentence.*

1 I'm surprised .... you. You're not normally as rude as you were tonight.
   A by   B for   C with   D at

2 Her divorce was a(n) .... experience for her and she still hasn't fully recovered.
   A stunning   B staggering   C shattering   D amazing

3 By a(n) .... stroke of luck, she survived the crash.
   A amazing   B shocking   C shattering   D surprised

4 People were .... the terrible pictures of the crash victims in the newspapers.
   A shocked with   B startled for   C shocked by   D amazed of

5 She was .... the traffic in the city. She had never seen so many cars before.
   A amazed at   B surprised for   C astonished with   D surprised of

6 It was a very quiet night so the sudden noise of breaking glass .... me.
  A shattered B staggered C startled D jumped

7 The Sears Tower in Chicago is a .... 443 metres high.
  A speechless B surprising C staggering D shattering

8 We were all .... at how well she spoke English.
  A astonished B shattered C shocked D incredible

9 I'm still too .... his sudden outburst to know what to say.
  A stunned with B shattered at C stunned by D speechless by

10 A friend I hadn't seen for a long time rang me up, which was a very nice ....
  A shock B surprise C wonder D astonishment

11 I was .... by his lack of intelligence. I couldn't believe anyone could be so stupid.
  A shattered B staggered C speechless D startled

12 She was in .... for several days after the accident.
  A surprise B shatter C shock D wonder

13 I was .... when her face suddenly appeared at the window.
  A shattered B staggered C startled D jumped

14 He was .... the news that he was going to be made redundant.
  A shattered by B speechless by C shattered from D incredible at

15 It doesn't .... me that you got annoyed. I would have felt the same.
  A shatter B stagger C surprise D startle

16 He finished the job with .... speed.
  A shattering B astonishing C stunning D shocking

17 She hoped that her question might catch him off ....
  A unawares B guard C aback D defence

18 It's .... – not only do Steven and I have the same surname, but we also share the same birthday and both drive Fiat Pandas!
  A stunning B surprised C incredible D surprising

19 It .... me how she manages to put up with him.
  A amazes B startles C stuns D shatters

20 His reaction took me .... surprise.
  A off B for C by D in

21 It's .... how difficult it is, considering how easy it looks.
  A surprising B shocking C startling D stunning

21.2 *For each of the sentences below, write a new sentence as similar as possible in meaning to the original sentence, but using the word given. This word must not be altered in any way.*

EXAMPLE   It's no use arguing: I've made up my mind.
point

ANSWER   *There's no point in arguing; I've made up my mind.*
....

1 The offer to go and work in Brazil was a complete surprise.
blue

....

2 I'm not surprised that he's got money problems.
comes

....

3 I'm not at all surprised that he looks so miserable – I've just found out that he's lost his job.
wonder

....

4 The sudden noise surprised me.
jump

....

5 I was surprised by his rudeness.
aback

....

6 I don't get shocked easily.
shock

....

7 I wasn't expecting you, so I haven't tidied the house yet.
unawares

....

8 I was so surprised that I couldn't say anything.
speechless

....

9 I was shocked when my friends suddenly decided to leave the country.
shock

....

Unit 22 Want/Like/Dislike

Part 1

1 **to feel like** (sth/*doing* sth)
to want something because of the
way you are feeling at that time

What do you feel like doing tonight?/I don't feel like going out./I feel like a drink.

2 **to fancy** (sth/*doing* sth)
to feel like

I fancy going to a night club./I don't fancy seeing that film./Do you fancy a cup of tea?

3 **to be in the mood** (*for* sth/*for doing* sth/*to do* sth)
to feel like something; to have the right feeling for something

'Do you feel like going to see that film?' – 'No, I'm not in the mood.'/Let's sit down. I'm not in the mood to dance anymore./Let's go out, I'm in the mood for some fun./I wasn't in the mood for arguing, so I said nothing.

4 **I could do with** (sth)
I would very much like; I need

I could do with something to eat – I haven't eaten all day.

5 **to be dying** (*for* sth/*to do* sth)
to want something very much

I'm dying for a drink, I'm terribly thirsty./I'm dying to get home and see all my friends again.

6 **to be desperate** (*for* sth/*to do* sth)
to want or need something very much

I was desperate to go to bed because I was so tired./He's desperate for a job.

Part 2

1 **to be fond of**
a (sth/*doing* sth)
to like

I'm not very fond of chocolate./She's fond of giving orders.

b (s.o./sth)
to love in a gentle or sentimental way

Although I don't love him, I'm very fond of him./I'm fond of this car – it's always been very reliable.

2 **to be keen**
a (*on* sth/*on doing* sth)
to like very much; to be interested in something

I'm keen on this kind of work./I get the feeling that you're not keen on working here.

b (*to do* sth)
to want to do something very much

I wasn't keen to come at first, but now I'm glad I did./My father's keen for me to become a doctor.

3 **to be crazy about** (s.o./sth)
to like very much

He's crazy about opera and listens to it all the time.

4. **to admire** (s.o./sth *for* sth)
to like someone or something because of the special qualities or abilities that they have

I really admire people like him who give up everything to go and work with the poor./You can't help admiring her determination./I admire her for not giving up.

5 **admiration** (*for* s.o./sth)
the feeling of admiring

I've got nothing but admiration for him.

6 **to have a high opinion of** (s.o./
sth)
to think that someone or
something has excellent qualities;
to admire

Her teachers had a high opinion of her work.

7 **to think highly of** (s.o./sth)
to have a high opinion of someone
or something

*Her boss thinks highly of her because she's very good at
her job.*

8 **to think a lot of** (s.o./sth)
to have a high opinion of someone
or something

I've always thought a lot of her.

9 **to rave** (*about* sth)
to speak enthusiastically about
something; to describe something
as excellent

*They raved about the place that they went to on holiday./
The critics are all raving about his new film.*

10 **to be full of praise** (*for* s.o./sth)
to say that someone or something
has excellent qualities

*He was full of praise for your work, in fact he said it was
the best thing he'd ever seen.*

11 **to respect** (s.o./sth)
to consider that someone or
something is important and
deserves attention

*I don't like him much but I respect him because he's good
at his job./Much as I respect your point of view, I think
you're wrong.*

12 **respect** (*for* s.o./sth)
the belief that someone is
important and should be respected

*I listen to what my parents tell me because I have a great
deal of respect for them./You should treat other people's
property with respect.*

13 **to look up to** (s.o.)
to respect

He looks up to his older brother.

14 **affection** (*for* s.o.)
the feeling of being fond of
someone

*She has a lot of affection for her old school friends./She
looked at him with great affection.*

15 **taste** (*in* sth)
choice or preference in the things
that you like

*He's got very good taste in clothes./She's got terrible taste
in men./They've got plenty of money but they don't have
particularly expensive tastes.*

16 **to approve** (*of* sth/*of doing* sth)
to think that something is morally
right or acceptable

*Surely you don't approve of such terrible behaviour?/I
approve of your choice./She doesn't approve of people
getting drunk.*

17 **approval**
   the feeling or statement of
   approving

You don't need my approval to do anything – I'm not your father.

18 **to take to** (s.o./sth)
   to like immediately and
   instinctively

I took to them the moment that I met them, and we've been friends ever since.

Part 3

1 **to detest** (s.o./sth/*doing* sth)
   to dislike very much

I detest him; I think he's vile./I detest having to do the washing-up.

2 **to loathe** (s.o./sth/*doing* sth)
   to detest

I loathe people like that./I loathe driving on motorways.

3 **to despise** (s.o.)
   to detest someone because you
   think they have no good qualities

I despise him and I hope I never see him again.

4 **to have a low opinion of** (s.o./
   sth)
   to dislike and disapprove of

I have a low opinion of him because I don't think he's honest.

5 **not to think much of** (s.o./sth)
   to have a low opinion of

I don't think much of the food in this restaurant.

6 **contempt** (*for* s.o./sth)
   the feeling that someone or
   something is inferior and of no
   importance

He showed his contempt for me by ignoring me./She has contempt for people who are not as intelligent as she is.

7 **to disapprove** (*of* sth/*of doing* sth)
   to think that something is bad or
   morally wrong

She disapproves of people swearing.

8 **disapproval**
   the feeling or statement of
   disapproving

Despite her parents' disapproval she married him.

9 **to criticise** (s.o./sth (*for* sth/*for doing* sth))
   to say that you do not like
   something or someone's actions;
   to say that something is wrong

You're always criticising – isn't anything ever good enough for you?/He doesn't like it if you criticise him./The report severely criticises the Government for the way it handled the affair./She criticised him for talking too much.

10 **criticism**
   the act of criticising; a comment
   which criticises

I don't mind criticism as long as it's constructive./He made a few criticisms but generally he liked my work.

11 **to be critical** (*of* s.o./sth)
to criticise (quite strongly)

He was critical of my work and told me I would have to start again.

12 **to condemn** (s.o./sth)
to criticise very strongly; to say that someone or something is bad and unacceptable

The Government utterly condemns the people responsible for this horrific crime./I condemn violence of any kind.

13 **to find/pick fault** (*with* s.o./sth)
to be unnecessarily critical (often of small, unimportant things)

She picked fault with all kinds of things in my flat – even the colour of the walls./He's always finding fault with me.

14 **to pick on** (s.o.)
to choose one person in particular to criticise; to criticise unfairly

The boss is nice to everyone else, but for some reason he's always picking on me.

15 **to run/put** (s.o./sth) **down**
to criticise strongly; to say that someone or something does not deserve respect

You're always running yourself down – you should have more confidence./He never has anything good to say about our work – all he ever does is put it down.

16 **to go off** (s.o./sth)
to stop liking someone or something

I used to like this kind of music, but I've gone off it now./I don't know why we split up – I suppose I just went off him.

17 **to be overrated**
to be liked more than it should be (by people in general)

I think this city is overrated – everyone says it's wonderful but it isn't that good.

Unit 22 Exercises

22.1 *Choose the word or phrase (A, B, C or D) which best completes each sentence.*

1 He won't do anything without his parents' ....
   A respect   B admiration   C affection   D approval

2 Now that she's the boss, she thinks people should treat her with more ....
   A respect   B admiration   C praise   D approval

3 I .... your patience. I would have lost my temper a long time ago.
   A approve   B admire   C take to   D respect

4 She .... her boss, because he makes her life so difficult.
   A detests   B disapproves   C goes off   D puts out

5 I .... this place! I hope I never come here again.
   A loathe   B condemn   C despise   D put off

6 While most people support the ambulancemen's claim for higher wages, a lot of people ....
   strike action.
   A loathe   B condemn   C criticise   D find fault with

7 He can't stand any .... of his work.
   A disapproval   B condemnation   C criticism   D contempt

8 I've got nothing but .... for idiots like you!
   A disapproval   B condemnation   C criticism   D contempt

9 She shook her head in .... as I went to light another cigarette.
   A disapproval   B condemnation   C criticism   D contempt

10 Why must you always .... fault with me?
   A put   B make   C find   D run

22.2 *Finish each of the following sentences in such a way that it means exactly the same as the sentence printed before it.*

   EXAMPLE   Who owns that car?

   ANSWER   *Who does that car belong to?*

1 I need an early night.
   I could ....

2 She told me that it was wrong of me to leave early.
   She criticised ....

3 He really likes cars.
   He's crazy ....

4 I don't want to go to that party tonight.
   I don't feel ....

5 She doesn't think very highly of politicians.
   She's got a ....

6 I'd like to go somewhere else for a change.
   I fancy ....

7 A lot of men think that it's wrong for women to work.
   A lot of men disapprove ....

8 I really need a holiday.
   I'm desperate ....

22.3 *Fill each of the blanks with one suitable word.*

1 I didn't take .... her husband at all; in fact I found him quite cold.

2 He has always looked .... to his father.

3 He treats his wife quite badly, especially in the way he's always putting her .... in public.

4 Because he's smaller than all the other boys at school, he tends to get picked ....

5 Since seeing that horrible documentary about modern farming techniques, I've gone .... the idea of eating meat.

22.4 *For each of the sentences below, write a new sentence as similar as possible in meaning to the original sentence, but using the word given. This word must not be altered in any way.*

EXAMPLE   It's no use arguing: I've made up my mind.
          point
ANSWER   *There's no point in arguing; I've made up my mind.*

1 She likes children.
   fond

   ....

2 I didn't want a serious conversation.
   mood

   ....

3 They buy nice furniture.
   taste

   ....

4 I don't really like this kind of music.
   keen

   ....

5 They said they thought your cooking was wonderful.
   praise

   ....

6 She criticises other people's weaknesses.
   critical

   ....

7 I like her a lot.
   affection

   ....

8 I want to learn as much as I can.
   keen

   ....

9 They've been saying how wonderful the hotel was.
   raving

   ....

10 She has a high opinion of you.
   highly

   ....

11 I don't think that violence is right in any circumstances.
   approve

   ....

12 I really want to see her again.
   dying

   ....

13 I have a high opinion of him.
   lot

   ....

14 I don't think that the film is as good as people say it is.
   overrated

   ....

15 I didn't think the restaurant was very good.
   much

   ....

16 She has a very low opinion of him.
   despises

   ....

Unit 23 Worried/Nervous

Part 1

1 **worried** (*about* s.o./sth)
unhappy because of being unable to stop thinking about a problem or possible problem

I'm worried about her – she hasn't been looking very well lately./People are becoming more and more worried about all the damage we are doing to the environment./She's worried about finding somewhere to live.

2 **to worry**
a (*about* s.o./sth)
to be worried

She worries all the time./Don't worry about me. I can look after myself.

b (s.o.)
to cause someone to be worried

It worries me that he hasn't phoned in over two months.

3 **worrying**
causing you to worry

Doctors have described the rapid spread of the disease as worrying.

4 **worry**
the uncomfortable feeling caused by being worried

All this worry is making her ill.

5 **a worry**
something that causes you to worry

John lost his job last week, so money is quite a worry for us at the moment.

6 **nervous** (*about* sth)
worried and slightly frightened (because you think that something is going to be terrible or because you are in a dangerous situation)

I'm nervous about the interview tomorrow./She gets nervous when she's in the house on her own.

7 **tense**
a under mental or emotional pressure; unable to relax

You seem rather tense – is anything the matter?/Pressure of work has made her very tense recently.

b causing you to feel nervous and unable to relax

The atmosphere was rather tense. Nobody really knew what was going to happen next.

8 **anxious**
a (*about* s.o./sth)
nervous, worried or troubled

I'm anxious about her – she hasn't phoned me for weeks.

b worrying

Father's illness was an anxious time for all of us.

9 **concerned** (*about* s.o./sth)
worried (especially about people or things that you care about)

She's concerned about his health.

10 **concern**
worry

There has been growing concern about the state of our prisons./Now that he's unemployed, finding another job is his main concern.

11 **bothered** (*about* s.o./sth)
worried

I wouldn't get so bothered about such a trivial matter if I were you.

12 **to bother**
   a (s.o.)
   to cause someone to be worried or concerned

You look worried – is something bothering you?/It bothers me what other people are saying about me.

   b (*about* s.o./sth)
   to be concerned about someone or something

Forget him. He's not worth bothering about.

   Note: **It doesn't bother me/I'm not bothered** = I don't mind

It doesn't bother me if he comes or not./I'm not bothered where we go.

13 **to have** (sth) **on your mind**
to be worried about a problem and be unable to stop thinking about it

She looks worried. She must have something on her mind./ He's had a lot on his mind recently.

14 **worked up** (*about* sth)
very worried, upset or angry, often about a particular thing that has happened

Don't get worked up about it – it's not important.

15 **wound up**
tense, often about a particular thing that has happened

He got very wound up because he thought he had offended her.

16 **flustered**
nervous and confused (especially because you have too many things to do at one time and therefore cannot cope or concentrate)

There were so many impatient customers waiting to be served that the shop assistant was getting more and more flustered.

17 **harassed**
worried and annoyed, especially because too many demands are made of you

You look harassed. Have a break.

18 **hectic**
(of a situation or a period of time) extremely busy and involving a lot of activity, so that you are unable to relax

It's been a hectic day and I'm exhausted.

19 **nerve-racking**
causing you to feel very tense and worried

Driving in a big city for the first time can be somewhat nerve-racking.

20 **hysterical**
in a state of hysteria

He became hysterical when they told him his wife had been killed.

21 **hysteria**
a powerful and uncontrollable state, especially of nervous excitement, anger or panic

There was hysteria when the passengers were told the plane was going to crash.

22 **to panic**
to be affected by a sudden and uncontrollable feeling of fear or worry, in such a way that you are unable to act sensibly

He panicked when he lost his five-year-old daughter in the crowd./Don't panic! I'm sure they'll be here soon.

23 **panic**
the state or feeling of sudden and uncontrollable fear or worry (especially affecting a whole group of people)

There was panic when someone shouted 'Fire!'/He's in a panic because he's only got two days left to finish the job.

24 **uncomfortable**
slightly nervous or embarrassed, especially in front of people or in particular situations

He looks at me in a peculiar way, which makes me feel uncomfortable.

25 **ill at ease**
uncomfortable, worried or anxious

She felt ill at ease at the party because she didn't know anyone.

26 **restless**
not wanting to stay still because you are anxious or bored

She gets restless when she's been in a job for more than a year.

27 **to fidget**
to make nervous, restless movements, especially with your hands or feet

He fidgeted in his chair while he was waiting for the interview.

Part 2

1 **pressure**
the demands (of your work or life style etc.) which cause you worry or difficulty

She left her job at the bank because she couldn't take the pressure./The pressure of university life is getting him down.

2 **under pressure**
suffering from pressure

It's not like him to lose his temper like that. I think he's been under a lot of pressure at work recently.

3 **tension**

a the feeling or state of being tense

There was fear and tension in her voice as she called out 'Who's there?'/Her headache was caused by tension.

b a tense atmosphere of possible danger, caused when relations between people are difficult

Weeks of increasing tension between the two countries finally erupted last night into war.

4 **strain**

tension and worry caused by pressure

The strain of having to bring up two young children on her own is beginning to show.

5 **a strain**

something that requires a great mental effort and causes you to feel tense

Trying to make conversation with people you don't like is a strain.

6 **stress**

mental, physical or emotional strain or tension, caused by pressure

I don't know if I could cope with the stress of living in London./In many cases stress can lead to heart attacks./He got fed up with the stresses and strains of city life and went to live in the country.

Unit 23 Exercises

23.1 *Choose the word or phrase (A, B, C or D) which best completes each sentence.*

1 She got rather .... because the recipe involved doing three things at once.
A restless   B concerned   C flustered   D bothered

2 I know it's not a big problem but it .... me and I want to sort it out.
A strains   B stresses   C presses   D bothers

3 He was such a powerful dictator that his speeches could produce .... in the crowds he spoke to.
A panic   B hysteria   C tension   D concern

4 I don't know why you're so .... about what happened. It's not that important.
A flustered   B bothered   C harassed   D worrying

5 This is a very .... period for them, because they are waiting for the doctor's report on their daughter's illness.
A nervous   B worried   C anxious   D bothered

6 I was so .... before the exam that I couldn't sleep.
A nervous   B uncomfortable   C worrying   D flustered

7 I felt .... because everyone was staring at me. I obviously wasn't welcome.
A uncomfortable   B anxious   C concerned   D bothered

8 There is considerable .... about his whereabouts, because he's been missing for several days.
A pressure   B strain   C concern   D stress

9 My father's illness is a .... I hope it doesn't get any worse.
A bother   B tension   C worry   D stress

10 The situation at work is extremely .... ; it seems I might lose my job.
   A bothering B concerning C worrying D wound up

11 Sport is one way of relieving the .... of a busy life.
   A tension B concern C bother D nerve

12 I'm not .... what we do tonight. It's entirely up to you.
   A concerned B nervous C bothered D anxious

13 News of possible war caused .... to spread throughout the country.
   A stress B strain C panic D pressure

14 She finds looking after the children a ....
   A stress B strain C pressure D tension

15 In the event of a fire, do not ....
   A fluster B harass C panic D fidget

16 After two hours the audience was beginning to get ....
   A restless B ill at ease C flustered D hectic

17 She became completely .... after the crash.
   A wound up B panicked C hysterical D harassed

18 The new trade agreement should help to reduce .... between the two governments.
   A stress B strain C pressure D tension

19 This has been an incredibly .... month.
   A hectic B flustered C wound up C harassed

20 You shouldn't .... so much. It's not good for you.
   A concern B worry C bother D fluster

21 I could tell he was nervous because he was .... in his chair.
   A flustering B fidgeting C harassing D fumbling

22 It was a very .... game – either team could have won.
   A nervous B concerned C tense D worried

23 She looks so much older than she really is. It must be due to ....
   A bother B worry C discomfort D tension

24 You'll have plenty of chances to retake your driving test, so don't get so .... about failing.
   A concerned B bothered C worked up D harassed

25 With half of the office either on holiday or ill, we're all feeling rather .... at the moment.
   A harassed B bothered C ill at ease D uncomfortable

26 The doctor says that she's suffering from .... and needs to take some time off work.
   A pressure B tension C strain D stress

23.2 *Fill each of the blanks with one suitable word.*

1 He always seems rather ill at .... in the company of strangers.

2 You know your problem? You get too wound .... about things.

3 I find I work best when I'm .... pressure.

4 I've got a lot .... my mind at the moment.

5 Making a speech in public for the first time can be a .... -racking experience.

6 He's very concerned .... the company's poor performance over the last few months.

Unit 24 Relaxed/Relieved

1 **relaxed**
not tense, worried or nervous

He's so relaxed that nothing seems to worry him.

2 **to relax**
a not to do anything which requires effort, work or concentration

After a week at work most people like to relax at the weekend.

b to become relaxed; to feel less tense, worried or nervous

Relax! We've got plenty of time to get to the airport.

3 **relaxing**
causing you to feel relaxed

This music is relaxing./It was a really relaxing holiday.

4 **relaxation**
the feeling of relaxing; a way of relaxing

I listen to music for relaxation.

5 **calm**
not being or not expressing that you are nervous, tense, angry or worried

Try to keep calm. The ambulance will be here soon./The situation is now much calmer, following yesterday's violent demonstrations.

6 **to calm down**
to become less nervous, tense or angry

I was nervous before the exam but I calmed down once it had started./Calm down! There's no need to get annoyed.

7 **cool**
calm and in control of your emotions

She always manages to stay cool under pressure.

8 **comfortable**
relaxed and confident, especially in front of people or in particular situations

I feel comfortable with people of my own age.

9 **at ease**
comfortable; without any feeling of worry

The interview started with a friendly chat to make the candidate feel at ease.

10 **to make yourself at home**
to feel at ease in someone else's house (usually used in the imperative as an invitation to behave as you would in your own home)

Come in! Sit down and make yourself at home!

11 **to unwind**
to relax after a tense and busy time

I like to listen to music – it helps me to unwind after a busy day.

12 **to take it/things easy**
   to relax and not do too much

Take it easy! There's nothing to worry about./The doctor said I should take things easy for a while until I'm fully recovered.

13 **to take** (sth) **in your stride**
   to react calmly to a difficult
   situation, as if it were not a
   problem

When she lost her job she took it in her stride./She seems to take examinations in her stride.

14 **relieved**
   no longer worried or anxious
   (because something ceases to be a
   problem)

I was so relieved when the doctor told me it was nothing serious./You'll be relieved to know that we've found your daughter.

15 **relief**
   the feeling of happiness caused by
   being relieved

Much to my relief, she said yes./It was a relief to leave that terrible job./These pills should bring you some relief.

16 **to breathe a sigh of relief**
   to make a sound in expression of
   relief

It was a terrible flight and I breathed a sigh of relief when the plane landed.

17 **to comfort** (s.o.)
   to make someone feel less
   worried or upset

She was crying so I talked to her about the problem in order to comfort her.

18 **comforting**
   able to comfort you

His kind words were comforting.

19 **comfort**
   the feeling of relief from worry or
   unhappiness; someone or
   something that brings this feeling

In the few hours before his death, he found great comfort in prayer./Throughout the crisis my family's support was a comfort to me.

20 **to assure** (s.o. *that* ...)
   to cause someone to feel sure or
   certain by telling them that they
   have no need to worry

I was worried that they wouldn't pay me but they assured me that they would.

21 **to reassure** (s.o. *that* ...)
   to make someone feel less
   worried and more confident, often
   by talking to them in a kind and
   friendly way

His words seemed to reassure her./She smiled as if to reassure him that everything would be all right.

Unit 24 Exercises

24.1 *Choose the word or phrase (A, B, C or D) which best completes each sentence.*

1 You're safe. What a(n) .... !
A comfort   B relief   C release   D assurance

2 Keep .... It's not the end of the world if we're a few minutes late.
A calm   B relaxed   C tranquil   D at ease

3 I can .... you that your illness is nothing to worry about.
A ensure   B insure   C assure   D make sure

4 .... ! There's no need to do all that work today.
A Calm   B Calm yourself   C Relax   D Relax yourself

5 He's always very .... , no matter what the problem.
A comfortable   B calmed down   C cool   D at ease

6 I've had a terrible day today. I just want to sit down, do nothing and ....
A relieve myself   B unwind   C relax myself   D calm

7 He seems very .... these days. He must be happy about the way things are going.
A relieved   B eased   C relaxed   D easy

8 Although they were strangers, their friendly manner made me feel .... immediately.
A comforted   B relieved   C easy   D at ease

9 She was so upset by the terrible news that nothing could .... her.
A assure   B relax   C relieve   D comfort

10 A weekend in the countryside is very .... after a hard week in the city.
A assuring   B relaxing   C relieving   D comforting

11 .... ! There's nothing to get upset about.
A Calm   B Unwind   C Tranquil   D Calm down

24.2 *The word in capitals at the end of each of the following sentences can be used to form a word that fits suitably in the blank space. Fill each blank in this way.*

EXAMPLE We had an interesting *discussion* about football.   DISCUSS

1 I don't feel particularly .... talking to people I've never met before.   COMFORT

2 I wasn't looking forward to the journey, so I was .... when it was over safely.
RELIEF

3 I thought he'd forgotten his promise, but he phoned to .... me
that nothing had changed.   SURE

4 I enjoy going on long walks for a bit of ....   RELAX

5 It's .... to know that when we retire, we will receive a very good pension.
COMFORT

24.3 *For each of the sentences below, write a new sentence as similar as possible in meaning to the original sentence, but using the word given. This word must not be altered in any way.*

EXAMPLE   It's no use arguing: I've made up my mind.
    point

ANSWER   *There's no point in arguing; I've made up my mind.*
....

1 Her friends' messages of sympathy helped her during her illness.
comfort

....

2 Please behave in my house as you would in your own house.
make

....

3 He deals calmly with everything.
stride

....

4 Why don't you relax for a few days and let me look after the shop?
easy

....

5 She was very relieved when she realised that her bag hadn't been stolen.
breathed

....

Section C
Characteristics

Units 25-35

Unit 25 Attractive/Good-looking

1 **attractive**
causing someone to like, want or be interested in someone or something

You don't have to be beautiful to be attractive./What an attractive house!/It's an attractive offer.

2 **to attract** (s.o.)
to cause someone to like, want or be interested in someone or something

What really attracted me to this place was the peace and quiet./Physically he doesn't attract me at all.

3 **to be attracted** (*to* s.o./sth)
to like and be interested in someone or something

I was attracted to her by her sense of humour./I'm not at all attracted to a career in banking.

4 **attraction**
the action or power of attracting

Why do so many people smoke? What's the attraction?

5 **(to be able) to see the attraction** (*of* sth)
to understand why other people like something

I can't see the attraction of living in a big city.

6 **good-looking**
physically attractive (of people)

She was very good-looking when she was young./Who was that good-looking man I saw you with last night?

7 **beautiful**
very attractive (usually of women, places or things)

She's beautiful./What a beautiful necklace!/The countryside was beautiful./Hasn't he got a beautiful voice?

8 **pretty**
good-looking or attractive (usually of women, children or little things)

I wouldn't say she was beautiful, but she's quite pretty./ That's a pretty dress you're wearing./What a pretty little tune!

9 **lovely**
beautiful or pleasing (of people or things)

He's got really lovely eyes./Isn't it a lovely day?/Thank you very much – that was a lovely meal.

10 **appealing**
interesting and attractive (of things, ideas etc.)

She's got an appealing sense of humour./I find the idea of being rich very appealing./That cake looks appealing – could I try a small piece?

11 **to appeal** (*to* s.o.)
to be attractive to someone

That film doesn't appeal to me at all./I must say the idea of living in a hot country appeals to me.

12 **stunning**
very attractive or beautiful

You look stunning in that dress tonight!/The view of the mountains was stunning./It's a stunning film – the best I've seen this year.

13 **tempting**
attractive and inviting (often making you want something that you should not have)

The idea of taking the day off work and going to the beach is very tempting./'Have another cream cake, Elizabeth.' – 'No, thank you. It's very tempting, but honestly I'm on a diet.'

14 **to tempt**
a (s.o. *to* sth/s.o. *to do* sth)
to try to attract someone to do or have something (often something that they should not do or have)

Can I tempt you to another helping of ice cream?/The fact that he was smoking tempted me to have a cigarette.

b (s.o. *into doing* sth)
to attract and persuade someone actually to do something that they know they should not do

His friends tempted him into taking drugs.

15 **to be tempted** (*to do* sth)
to want to do something (often something that you should not do)

I was so poor that I was tempted to steal./She got me so angry that I was tempted to tell her exactly what I thought of her.

16 **a temptation**
something that tempts you

Although he was very rude, I managed to resist the temptation to hit him.

Unit 25 Exercises

25.1 *Choose the word or phrase (A, B, C or D) which best completes each sentence.*

1 What a(n) .... smell! What are you cooking?
A pretty   B lovely   C tempted   D attracting

2 It's an absolutely .... place to go for a holiday! You'll think you're in paradise.
A pretty   B beautiful   C good-looking   D appealing

3 Those ice-creams look .... Shall we have one?
A attracting   B tempting   C stunning   D good-looking

4 The cottages in the village were very .... , so I took a lot of photographs of them.
A attracted   B stunning   C good-looking   D pretty

5 She has a(n) .... personality, so most people like her.
A tempting   B attracting   C pretty   D attractive

6 The thought of taking the day off work is very ....
A good-looking   B lovely   C appealing   D stunning

7 He's very .... and a lot of the other girls in the school would like to go out with him.
A lovely   B stunning   C good-looking   D beautiful

8 The orchestra gave a(n) .... performance and received a standing ovation.
A stunning   B good-looking   C appealing   D pretty

9 That kind of work doesn't .... me. I think it would be very boring.
A appeal   B attract   C tempt   D appeal for

25.2 *Finish each of the following sentences in such a way that it means exactly the same as the sentence printed before it.*

EXAMPLE Who owns that car?

ANSWER *Who does that car belong to?*
....

1 People are persuaded by adverts to spend more than they can afford.
Adverts tempt ....

2 Older men attract her.
She is ....

3 I felt like walking out without paying because the service was so bad.
I was tempted ....

4 I find their lifestyle quite attractive, although I probably wouldn't really enjoy it.
Their lifestyle appeals ....

5 The dress was so tempting that I bought it.
I couldn't resist the ....

6 I don't know why people are attracted to spending all day on the beach.
I can't see the ....

Unit 26 Dependent/Independent

1 **to depend on**
  a (s.o./sth)
  to need in order to live, succeed
  or do something

As a charity, our work depends entirely on volunteers./The whole island depends on the tourist industry for its income.

  b (s.o./sth (*doing* sth/*to do* sth))
  to have confidence in, or put your
  trust in someone or something

I'm depending on them to lend me some money./If I were you, I wouldn't depend on the train being on time.

  c (s.o./sth)
  (not used in continuous tenses) to
  be influenced or dictated by

I might go tomorrow. It depends on the weather./She's not sure if she's coming – it depends on whether she can get a lift or not.

2 **depending on**
  dictated and influenced by

I might buy it, depending on how much it costs.

3 **dependent**
  a (*on* s.o./sth)
  unable to live or manage without
  someone or something (physically,
  financially or emotionally)

She's got two dependent children./He's dependent on his parents for money./She's dependent on the drugs that the doctor prescribes her.

  b (*on* sth)
  dictated or decided by something

The amount of tax you pay is dependent on your salary.

4 **to rely on**
  a (s.o./sth)
  to need someone or something,
  and be dependent on them

He can't look after himself. He relies entirely on his mother./I wish I didn't have to rely on the bus for getting me to work.

  b (s.o./sth (*doing* sth/*to do* sth))
  to trust or have confidence in
  someone or something (to do what
  you want them to do, or to be as
  you want them to be)

We can't rely on our car – it keeps breaking down./You can rely on her to keep a secret./I was relying on that cheque arriving today, but it didn't.

5 **to count on** (s.o./sth (*doing* sth/*to do* sth))
  to trust or expect (that someone
  will do what you want them to
  do, or that something will be as
  you want it to be)

You can't count on him – he's always breaking his promises./It's such a shame – she was really counting on passing that exam./I'm counting on you to help me./We were counting on the weather being sunny, so neither of us had taken our coats.

6 **to bank on** (s.o./sth (*doing* sth/*to do* sth))
  to count on

We're banking on your help./When he left his job he was banking on getting another one easily.

7 **to let** (s.o.) **down**
  to disappoint someone by failing
  to do what they were relying on
  you to do

He's always letting me down – we arrange to meet and then he cancels at the last moment./She feels that she has let her parents down by failing all her exams.

8 **independent**
  a not needing other people or things

She left home because she wanted to be independent.

  b (*of* s.o./sth) without the help of; without being influenced by

She made her own decision, independent of any advice.

9 **independence**
  the state of being independent

I don't want to get married because I don't want to give up my independence.

10 **free**
  a (*to do* sth) able to do what you want to do

I want to be free to make my own decisions./You're free to go wherever you like.

  b (*from/of* sth) without; not worried or influenced by

It's nice to be free of money problems./I'd love to be free from all these responsibilities.

11 **freedom**
  a independence; the state of being free

They allow their children too much freedom./They're fighting for their freedom.

  b the power or right to act, say, think etc. as you please

I want the freedom to make my own decisions./Freedom of speech is a fundamental right in a democratic country.

12 **liberated**
  free from traditional ideas, particularly in social or sexual matters

She's a liberated woman./They lead a very liberated lifestyle.

13 **to fend for yourself**
  to look after yourself without relying on other people for help

He's had to fend for himself ever since he left home at the age of sixteen.

14 **on your own**
  alone; without help from anyone else

She lives on her own./Nobody helped me – I did it on my own.

15 **by yourself**
  on your own

I spent the whole weekend by myself./Are you sure you can do it by yourself?

Unit 26 Exercises

26.1 *Choose the word or phrase (A, B, C or D) which best completes each sentence.*

1 She's become a lot more .... and no longer needs everything to be done for her.
   A free   B single   C independent   D by herself

2 There is too much work for me to do ....
   A by my own   B on myself   C by myself   D for my own

3 We're depending .... you to come.
   A of   B from   C on   D by

4 She wanted to be free .... the influence of her parents.
   A on   B from   C for   D without

5 As a single person, my .... is very important to me.
   A liberation   B independence   C liberty   D emancipation

6 Both she and her partner have got .... attitudes towards marriage.
   A single   B free   C independent   D liberated

7 The price of the coach tickets .... on how many people want to go.
   A relies   B depends   C counts   D banks

8 The press were given complete .... to photograph any part of the military base.
   A freedom   B independence   C liberation   D liberty

9 Whether or not you need a visa .... on which country you come from.
   A counts   B relies   C is dependent   D is depending

10 She left home to be independent .... her parents.
   A from   B on   C of   D for

26.2 *For each of the sentences below, write a new sentence as similar as possible in meaning to the original sentence, but using the word given. This word must not be altered in any way.*

   EXAMPLE   It's no use arguing: I've made up my mind.
   point

   ANSWER   *There's no point in arguing; I've made up my mind.*

1 When she left home, she had to do everything on her own.
   fend

   ....

2 If you leave this job, don't assume that you'll get another one.
   count

   ....

3 I may go out tonight but it depends on how long my homework takes me.
   depending

   ....

4 I'm expecting to be promoted soon.
   banking

   ....

5 Most university students need the financial support of their parents.
   depend

   ....

6 If I were you, I wouldn't trust the weather to be good.
   rely

   ....

7 Nobody helped me to build this.
own

....

8 I don't want anything to stop me from enjoying myself.
free

....

9 I don't want to have to need other people.
dependent

....

10 Her income is vital to them.
rely

....

11 Our car is extremely reliable; it hasn't disappointed us once in the last ten years.
let

....

Unit 27 Different/Similar

Part 1

1 **different** (*to/from* s.o./sth)
not the same

Although they are sisters they're very different to each other./His political views are different from mine.

2 **no different** (*to/from* s.o./sth)
the same

His problems are no different to anyone else's./Today was no different from any other day.

3 **a difference** (*in* sth/*between* two things)
the way in which one thing is different from another

There was a big difference in price so we had to buy the smaller one./What's the difference between this word and that word?/There's absolutely no difference between the two words.

4 **a subtle difference**
a small but important difference

There is a subtle difference between enjoying food and being greedy.

5 **to be able to tell the difference** (*between* two things)
to know that there is a difference

I can't tell the difference between cheap wine and expensive wine.

6 **to distinguish** (*between* two things/sth *from* sth else)
to see, hear, understand etc. the difference

I can't distinguish between blue and green./I can't distinguish blue from green./I find it difficult to distinguish one accent from another.

7 **distinctive**
clearly different from anything else

His music has a distinctive sound./She wears very distinctive clothes.

8 **to stand out**
to be distinctive, or easy to notice

She stood out in the crowd because of the bright colours she was wearing.

9 **the opposite** (*of* s.o./sth)
the person or thing that is as different as possible from something else

'Different' is the opposite of 'the same'./He's very hard-working, but his brother is just the opposite.

10 **to contrast**
a (sth *with* sth *else*)
to compare two things in order to look at or show the differences between them

It's interesting to contrast the attitudes of different people./If we contrast this year's figures with last year's, you'll all see that sales have increased dramatically.

b (*with* sth)
to be very different from

His actions contrast with his opinions.

11 **as opposed to**
rather than (used when you are contrasting two things in order to emphasise the first thing and show that there is a clear difference)

We're looking for someone with experience as opposed to qualifications.

12 **to vary** to be different at different times or in different circumstances	*The amount of work I do varies from day to day./The shirts vary in price from £15 to £40./Salaries vary according to age, qualifications and experience.*
13 **various** several different; of different kinds	*I've got various interests including music, reading and sport./The police were given various accounts of what had happened.*
14 **a variety** (*of* sth) a number of different kinds of the same thing	*I've got a variety of friends./There's a whole variety of reasons why I don't like her.*

Part 2

1 **similar** (*to* s.o./sth) almost the same	*Their house is similar to the one I live in./They're very similar in size.*
2 **alike** similar (in appearance, character etc.)	*They're so alike that you would think they were sisters.*
3 **identical** (*to* s.o./sth) exactly the same	*That necklace looks identical to the one I lost./They're identical twins, so people are always confusing them.*
4 **equivalent** (*to* sth) equal to or corresponding to (in value, amount, meaning etc.)	*What is £20 equivalent to in Japanese yen?/First prize is either a holiday for two in Florida, or an equivalent amount in cash.*
5 **an equivalent** (*of* sth) something that is equivalent to something else	*An inch is the equivalent of 2.54 centimetres./Is there an equivalent of the Financial Times in Italy?*
6 **to amount to the same thing** to produce the same result; to mean the same	*If you pay this bill for me and I pay the next one for you, it amounts to the same thing./She didn't actually say no, but it amounted to the same thing.*
7 **to even out** to become equal; to balance in the end	*I paid for some things and she paid for some things, but it evened out because we both spent the same amount.*
8 **a thin line** (*between* two things) a very small difference between two extremes	*There is a thin line between being careful with money and being mean.*
9 **to split hairs** to insist on very small differences which are unimportant	*'You were an hour late.' – 'No, I was only 59 minutes late.' – 'Don't split hairs.'*

Unit 27 Exercises

27.1 *Choose the word or phrase (A, B, C or D) which best completes each sentence.*

1 Sometimes I pay and sometimes she pays, but it all .... in the end.
   A amounts   B evens out   C stands out   D balances

2 What's .... this word?
   A opposite from   B contrary to   C the contrary of   D the opposite of

3 He .... because he was the only old person there.
   A contrasted   B stood up   C varied   D stood out

4 It's funny you should say that. I've just had the .... thought.
   A like   B identical   C alike   D similar

5 House prices .... greatly from one area to the next.
   A contrast   B vary   C distinguish   D stand out

6 This particular flower is famous for its .... smell.
   A distinguished   B differential   C distinctive   D different

7 I had .... temporary jobs when I was a student.
   A different   B distinctive   C various   D varying

8 We sell a .... of different wines from around the world.
   A variation   B variety   C variance   D variant

9 The two pictures are very .... , but if you look carefully, you'll notice one or two differences.
   A identical   B equal   C same   D alike

10 Eighty kilometres is the .... fifty miles.
   A equivalent of   B equivalent from   C equal of   D equal from

11 Although technically speaking he wasn't sacked, it .... the same thing.
   A evens out to   B amounts to   C points to   D signifies

27.2 *For each of the sentences below, write a new sentence as similar as possible in meaning to the original sentence, but using the word given. This word must not be altered in any way.*

EXAMPLE   It's no use arguing: I've made up my mind.
          point

ANSWER   *There's no point in arguing; I've made up my mind.*

1 The original painting and the copy look the same to me.
   tell

   ....

2 I don't want to point out a trivial little difference, but your facts aren't quite right.
   split

   ....

3 What he earns in a week is the same as what I earn in a month.
   equivalent

   ....

4 The way he behaves in private is very different from the way he behaves at work.
   contrasts

....

5 This record is exactly the same as the last one they made.
   different

....

6 Parents try to teach their children to understand that right and wrong are two different things.
   distinguish

....

7 This programme is like one that used to be on years ago.
   similar

....

8 I prefer playing football rather than watching it.
   opposed

....

9 Being mean and being careful with money are not quite the same.
   subtle

....

10 Not having much money is not the same as being completely broke.
   different

....

11 His attitude has been different recently.
   difference

....

12 Some people say that there's hardly any difference between love and hate.
   line

....

Unit 28 Friend

1 **a good friend**
someone who you know very well and like very much

He's a good friend of mine./She was my best friend at school – we did everything together.

2 **a close friend**
an intimate friend who you can trust

She's a close friend – I can discuss anything with her.

3 **an old friend**
a friend who you have known for a long time

Gary and I are old friends – we went to the same school together.

4 **a friendship**
a relationship between friends

I'm not going to argue with him about this because I value our friendship too much.

5 **a mate**
(*colloquial, usually used by men*)
a friend

I've got a mate who's a mechanic – if you like, I'll ask him to look at your car./He's my best mate.

6 **an acquaintance**
someone who you know slightly, but who is not a close friend

She seems to have a lot of acquaintances, but not very many friends.

7 **a colleague**
someone who you work with

You were in a meeting when I rang, so I spoke to one of your colleagues.

8 **to be friends** (*with* s.o.)
to have a friendship with someone

Are you still friends with him?/We've been friends for ten years.

9 **to make friends** (*with* s.o.)
to form a friendship with someone

She finds it easy to make friends./Have you made friends with anyone from work yet?

10 **to get to know** (s.o.)
to find out what someone is like

She seems really nice – I'd like to get to know her better.

11 **to get on (well)** (*with* s.o.)
to have a friendly relationship with someone

David and I don't get on./I've always got on very well with my parents.

12 **to be on good/friendly terms**
(*with* s.o.)
to have a friendly relationship with someone

I never realised that you and Roy were on such friendly terms./Although he's left the company, he's still on good terms with them.

13 **to go out** (*with* s.o.)
to have a romantic relationship with someone

They've been going out (together) for six months./I went out with her for over a year, but I don't see her nowadays.

14 **to fall out** (*with* s.o.)
to stop being friends with
someone because of a
disagreement

They fell out with each other over some stupid argument.

15 **to break up/split up** (*with* s.o.)
to separate; to end a relationship
or marriage

Sally has just broken up with Nick./Sally and Nick have just split up.

Unit 28 Exercises

28.1 *Fill each of the blanks with one suitable word.*

1 I hardly know him. He's just an .... of mine.

2 I bumped into an .... friend the other day. I hadn't seen her for ages.

3 He's one of my ...., but I don't know him very well. I only work with him.

4 I know her very well. She's a .... friend of mine.

5 He was my .... friend at school, so it's strange how we don't get on at all these days.

6 Their .... is very important to me, so I hope we will always be friends.

28.2 *For each of the sentences below, write a new sentence as similar as possible in meaning to the original sentence, but using the word given. This word must not be altered in any way.*

EXAMPLE   It's no use arguing: I've made up my mind.
          point

ANSWER   *There's no point in arguing; I've made up my mind.*
         ....

1 I have a friendly relationship with everyone at work.
  terms

  ....

2 We found out a lot about each other during the journey.
  know

  ....

3 She has a friendly relationship with most people.
  gets

  ....

4 Have you become anyone's friend since you arrived?
  made

  ....

5 He's stopped being friends with Clare.
  fallen

  ....

6 Have you heard the news? Roger has separated from Diana.
  split

  ....

7 He's been her boyfriend for about three weeks.
   going

   ....

8 They separated last month.
   broke

   ....

9 I used to be a friend of his.
   with

   ....

Unit 29 Funny

1 **funny**
causing you to laugh or smile

That's the funniest thing I've heard for a long time./He's a very funny man.

2 **amusing**
funny

It's not the funniest film I've ever seen, but it's quite amusing./She's always very amusing.

3 **to amuse** (s.o.)
to seem funny to someone and cause them to laugh or smile

His stories amused the children./I thought it was funny but no one else was amused.

4 **hilarious**
extremely funny; causing you to laugh a lot

It's a hilarious film – go and see it!/He told me some hilarious jokes – I couldn't stop laughing.

5 **hysterical**
hilarious

I must tell you what happened today – it was hysterical!

6 **witty**
amusing in a clever way (especially involving the clever use of words)

The chairman's speech was very witty.

7 **sense of humour**
the ability to be funny or to understand what is funny

I like her sense of humour – she makes me laugh./I don't really like the American sense of humour./Don't look so miserable – where's your sense of humour?

8 **a joke**
something that is said or done to make people laugh

Have you heard the joke about the talking racehorse?/Has anybody got any good jokes?

9 **to tell** (s.o.) **a joke**

She's very good at telling jokes./Tell us a joke!

10 **a dirty joke**
a joke about sex etc. (which could offend)

They got drunker and drunker and the jokes got dirtier and dirtier.

11 **a sick joke**
a tasteless joke about disease, death, tragedy etc.

I think he upset quite a lot of people with that sick joke about the plane crash.

12 **a standing joke**
a joke (usually about a particular person) which is often repeated among friends, family members or a particular group of people

His meanness has become a bit of a standing joke in our family.

13 **a practical joke**
a trick that is played on someone in order to make them appear ridiculous and amuse others

They hid his shoes as a practical joke.

14 **to play a practical joke** (*on* s.o.)   *His friends are always playing practical jokes on him. Last week they phoned him pretending to be the police.*

15 **to be joking/kidding**
to deliberately say something
untrue, in order to fool or surprise
someone, or to be funny

I was only joking when I said I wanted you to work late tonight./If you think I'm going to drive you fifty miles to the airport at three o'clock in the morning, you must be kidding!/'I've just won £10,000' – 'You're joking!' (= I don't believe you.)

16 **to laugh at** (s.o.)
to make jokes about someone who
you consider to be foolish or to
have done something foolish

People laugh at him because he wears such strange clothes./I'll only sing if you promise not to laugh at me.

17 **to make fun of** (s.o.)
to laugh at someone in an unkind
way so as to make them appear
foolish or ridiculous

Children can be very cruel in the way they make fun of anyone who's slightly different./She's always making fun of him because he's going bald.

18 **to tease** (s.o.)
to make jokes about someone in
order to try to embarrass them
(often between friends etc.)

His friends tease him about his accent./No, I don't really think your shirt is horrible – I'm only teasing.

19 **to pull someone's leg**
to tease someone by trying to
make them believe something that
is not true

'Is this really your car?' – 'No, I was pulling your leg. It belongs to my father.'/I can't believe he's only twenty-eight. You're pulling my leg, aren't you?

20 **to take the mickey** (*out of* s.o.):
(*colloquial*) to make fun of
someone, either in a friendly or
unkind way

All the other children take the mickey out of him, because he's no good at games.

21 **to burst out laughing**
to start laughing suddenly and
loudly

What he told me was so ridiculous that I burst out laughing.

22 **to laugh your head off**
to laugh loudly and for a long
time because you find something
very funny

She laughed her head off at his pathetic attempt to speak French.

23 **the punch line**
the last line of a joke (the part
that causes you to laugh)

I know it was a good joke, but I can't remember the punch line.

Unit 29 Exercises

29.1 *Choose the word or phrase (A, B, C or D) which best completes each sentence.*

1 Her awful singing is a .... joke at school.
   A dirty   B sick   C standing   D practical

2 He made a .... joke about the Ethiopian famine victims.
   A dirty   B sick   C standing   D practical

3 Have you heard the joke about the bishop and the actress? It's a bit ....
   A dirty   B sick   C standing   D practical

4 I haven't laughed so much in years. It was absolutely .... !
   A amusing   B hilarious   C funny   D diverting

5 He loves .... her about all her boyfriends.
   A teasing   B joking   C kidding   D pulling

6 I can't say I find his jokes particularly ....
   A enjoying   B amusing   C standing   D fun

29.2 *Fill each of the blanks with one suitable word.*

1 He ruined the joke by saying the .... line before the end.

2 When he told her what had happened she burst .... laughing.

3 He has a strange .... of humour and laughs at all sorts of peculiar things.

4 They .... a practical joke .... him by pouring vodka in his lemonade while he wasn't looking.

5 His friends make .... of him because he's got an enormous nose.

6 She .... me a very funny joke, but I can't remember it now.

29.3 *For each of the sentences below, write a new sentence as similar as possible in meaning to the original sentence, but using the word given. This word must not be altered in any way.*

EXAMPLE   It's no use arguing: I've made up my mind.
          point

ANSWER   *There's no point in arguing; I've made up my mind.*

1 You know I told you I was a millionaire? Well, I was teasing you.
  leg

  ....

2 Her jokes made us laugh very much.
  funny

  ....

3 Everybody made fun of him because he didn't know the answer.
  laughed

  ....

4 Her comments used words in a very clever and amusing way.
  witty

  ....

132

5 I don't believe you. He's not really your brother, is he?
kidding

....

6 It's a brilliant film – I laughed uncontrollably all the way through.
head

....

7 She obviously didn't find your jokes funny.
amused

....

8 Everybody made fun of him because he'd had his hair cut so short.
mickey

....

9 I was highly amused by her story.
hysterical

....

Unit 30 Important/Trivial

Part 1

1 **important**
   necessary; mattering a lot

   That's a very important point./It's important (for people) to be able to relax./It might not matter to you, but it's important to me./It's very important that you get this done by tomorrow.

2 **importance**
   the quality of being important; the reason why something is important

   Her work is of the greatest importance to the world of medicine./He doesn't see the importance of saving money – he'd much rather spend it.

3 **essential**
   extremely important and necessary

   Foreign travel is an essential part of my job./It's essential to study grammar if you want to speak the language correctly./It's essential that you don't tell anyone.

4 **vital**
   essential (for something to succeed, happen etc.)

   His work is vital to our success./It's vital that we get help to him immediately.

5 **crucial**
   very important (especially in causing the difference between success and failure)

   The first few months were a crucial time for the company.

6 **significant**
   a having a special meaning or importance (often leading to a belief or conclusion)

   It's significant that he didn't mention the subject./Do you think her absence could be significant?

   b important because of being large in quantity

   There has been a significant drop in my income recently.

7 **significance**
   importance or meaning; the quality of being significant

   What was the significance of his remark?/If I were you, I wouldn't attach any significance to what he said./We didn't talk about anything of significance.

8 **major**
   more important, in terms of seriousness, influence, size etc. (in comparison with other things)

   Drugs are a major problem in modern society./Money was a major reason why I took the job.

9 **main**
   most important, in terms of seriousness, influence, size etc.

   The main reason why I changed my job was boredom./His main problem at the moment is money./Be careful crossing the main road.

10 **valuable**
    very useful; of great help

    It was a valuable experience because I learnt a lot from my mistake.

11 **invaluable**
    extremely valuable

    Your help during this last week has been invaluable.

12 **basic**
simple and important; on which
everything else depends

There is a basic difference between our attitudes, so we'll never agree.

13 **fundamental**
basic

An understanding of the grammar and structure of a language is fundamental to your progress in that language.

14 **above all**
most importantly

You have to be clever to succeed, but above all you have to be lucky.

15 **a priority**
something that you think is more
important or needs more urgent
attention than other things

My priority is to find somewhere to live first, and then I can start thinking about getting a job./You need to get your priorities right and not waste time doing things that don't matter.

16 **to take** (s.o./sth) **seriously**
to believe that someone or
something is important and
deserves attention or respect

I take it seriously if someone accuses me of being dishonest./She takes her work very seriously./I'm afraid I can't take him seriously.

17 **to feel strongly** (*about* sth/*that* ...)
to have strong opinions about
something

He obviously felt strongly about the subject, because he lost his temper./I feel strongly that our immigration laws should be changed.

18 **to live for** (sth)
to consider something to be the
most important thing in your life

He lives for his work.

19 **to stress** (sth/*that* ...)
to say or indicate strongly that
something is important

He stressed that he didn't want to cause any trouble./He stressed the need for greater co-operation between the police and the public.

20 **to emphasise** (sth/*that* ...)
to stress

He repeated himself to emphasise that he wasn't joking./As a doctor, I can't emphasise enough the importance of regular exercise.

21 **to boil down to** (sth)
(of a situation, argument,
statement etc.) to have as its main
issue

The details don't matter. What it boils down to is whether it's possible or not./What the argument really seems to boil down to is money.

Part 2

1 **trivial**
unimportant and uninteresting

There's no point arguing about something as trivial as that.

2 **minor**
not important (in comparison with
other things)

It's a minor problem, nothing to get worried about.

3 **to make light of** (sth)
to indicate that something (a
problem etc.) is not important

*He made light of his money problems – he said they would
get better soon.*

4 **to laugh** (sth) **off**
to try to make something (a
problem etc.) seem unimportant,
by joking about it

*'Was he very upset about losing his job?' – 'Not at all, he
just laughed it off.'*

5 **to shrug** (sth) **off**
to treat something (a problem etc.)
as not important or serious

*She shrugged off her disappointment and continued as if
nothing had happened.*

6 **to play** (sth) **down**
to try to make people think that
something is less important than it
really is

The Government is playing down the economic crisis.

7 **so what?**
(*colloquial*) an expression
meaning 'why should I care?'
(used to indicate that you do not
consider something to be
important)

*'You were very rude to those people.' – 'So what? I'll
never see them again.'/So what if he doesn't like me? I
don't like him either.*

Unit 30 Exercises

30.1 *Choose the word or phrase (A, B, C or D) which best completes each sentence.*

1 His help was .... to the success of the business.
A main   B crucial   C basic   D major

2 It was only a(n) .... remark. I don't see why you're taking it so seriously.
A minor   B invaluable   C fundamental   D trivial

3 There's a .... difference between our two cultures.
A crucial   B special   C fundamental   D main

4 He suffered relatively .... injuries.
A trivial   B basic   C minor   D weak

5 The .... problem with the flat is that it is too small.
A important   B significant   C vital   D main

6 We don't want to have to carry a lot of luggage, so only pack the most .... items.
A essential   B main   C crucial   D significant

7 It's .... that he didn't go to his son's wedding.
A important   B significant   C crucial   D essential

8 She is a .... British writer.
A main   B major   C crucial   D vital

9 He's a(n) .... friend to me.
A significant   B vital   C invaluable   D main

10 The .... ingredient of bread is flour.
   A valuable   B significant   C crucial   D basic

11 We are grateful to Mrs Price for her many years of .... service.
   A essential   B crucial   C fundamental   D valuable

30.2 *Fill each of the blanks with one suitable word.*

1 The actress shrugged .... the bad reviews.

2 Success often boils .... to luck.

3 I care about my job and my friends, but .... all, I care about my family.

4 The chairman played .... the company's financial problems.

5 So .... if she's ten years older than I am? I still intend to marry her.

30.3 *For each of the sentences below, write a new sentence as similar as possible in meaning to the original sentence, but using the word given. This word must not be altered in any way.*

   EXAMPLE   It's no use arguing: I've made up my mind.
             point

   ANSWER   *There's no point in arguing; I've made up my mind.*

1 Don't you understand that it's important to be more careful?
importance

....

2 'Don't forget, it's only my opinion,' he said.
stressed

....

3 I wish you'd accept that this is important.
seriously

....

4 What did his silence mean?
significance

....

5 He pretended that his latest business failure was not important.
laughed

....

6 Football is the most important thing in his life.
lives

....

7 My opinions on religion are not very strong.
strongly

....

8 You must see a doctor as soon as possible.
   vital

   ....

9 I want you to understand very clearly that I'm not criticising you.
   emphasise

   ....

10 It's time you realised what's important and what isn't.
   priorities

   ....

11 He said that the crisis wasn't important.
   light

   ....

Unit 31 Luck/Chance/Coincidence

Part 1

1 **luck**
   a something that seems to be affected by chance and that causes good or bad things to happen to a person

   It's a game of luck rather than skill./When I got to the station, the train had already left – that's typical of my luck.

   b success resulting from chance; good fortune

   I couldn't believe my luck when I realised that mine was the winning ticket./She shook his hand and wished him luck.

2 **lucky**
   having, bringing or resulting from good luck; not resulting from planning, effort or ability

   I was lucky to find such a good flat so quickly./That's the second nice thing that's happened today – it must be my lucky day./It was lucky that a train came so soon – I might have been late otherwise.

3 **luckily**
   because of good luck

   A car nearly hit me. Luckily, the driver stopped in time.

4 **with (a bit of) luck**

   With (a bit of) luck, I'll have enough money to go on holiday soon.

5 **a piece/stroke of luck**
   something lucky

   Meeting him was a piece of luck because he told me about this wonderful place./'How did you know where to find us?' – 'We didn't; it was a stroke of luck.'

6 **good luck!/best of luck!**
   expressions used to wish someone success

   Good luck in the exam tomorrow!/Best of luck in the interview!

7 **unlucky**
   having, bringing or resulting from bad luck

   The team were unlucky to lose./Some people think it's unlucky to walk under a ladder.

8 **bad luck!/hard luck!**
   expressions used to show sympathy towards someone who has been unlucky or disappointed etc.

   'I failed the exam.' – 'Bad luck!'/'I didn't get the job.' – 'Hard luck!'

9 **fortunate**
   lucky (particularly in view of the circumstances)

   It's fortunate that I brought some extra money with me./He's fortunate to be alive, considering how bad his injuries were.

10 **fortunately**
   luckily

   Fortunately for her, the burglars took nothing of any real value.

11 **unfortunate**

   a unlucky

He's been rather unfortunate in his choice of business partners./It's a shame you didn't win – you were unfortunate, that's all.

   b causing you to feel sorry; inappropriate

It was a most unfortunate remark./It's unfortunate that you couldn't have told me all this before.

12 **unfortunately**

it is/was sad or disappointing (that ...); I'm afraid (that ...)

I'd like to see you. Unfortunately, I'm busy./I sympathise with your complaint but unfortunately there's nothing I can do about it.

13 **fate**

the power that is thought to control and dictate everything that happens, in a way that humans are unable to change or stop

It must have been fate that I was offered a job just when I was thinking of leaving mine.

14 **by chance**

without having been planned

Someone at the party gave me a lift home because by chance they lived in the same street.

15 **a fluke**

a piece of accidental good luck, involving no skill at all

I don't know how I won the game – it was a fluke.

16 **a break**

a lucky opportunity that results in success

His main break came when he entered a local talent competition, where sitting in the audience was the head of a large record company.

17 **a coincidence**

a happening by chance of two or more things at the same time or in the same place, in a surprising way

It was a coincidence that we were both in the same bar at the same time – I had no idea he would be there./By an amazing coincidence they not only share the same birthday, but they both have husbands called Timothy.

18 **to coincide** (*with* sth)

to happen at the same time

My final exam coincides with my birthday.

19 **to bump/run into** (s.o.)

to meet someone by chance

I bumped into a friend in the street./Guess who I ran into this morning?

20 **all being well**

as long as nothing unlucky happens

All being well, I'll have saved enough money by next year to buy a new car.

21 **to happen** (*to do* sth)

to do something as a result of chance or coincidence

We just happened to be passing, so we thought we'd come and say hello./If you happen to see her, will you give her this message.

Unit 31 Exercises

31.1 *Choose the word or phrase (A, B, C or D) which best completes each sentence.*

1 .... luck! I hope everything goes well for you in the future.
   A Best   B Better   C Best of   D Fine

2 The goal was a .... – I was trying to pass the ball, not to score!
   A coincidence   B break   C fluke   D chance

3 By .... my brother is travelling on the same flight as me.
   A fate   B fortune   C break   D coincidence

4 ....! I hope you win.
   A Have luck   B Good luck   C Good chance   D Good fortune

5 It was a .... finding somewhere so nice to live.
   A good luck   B good chance   C chance   D piece of luck

6 Getting the part of Hamlet at the National Theatre was the .... he'd been waiting for.
   A fluke   B break   C coincidence   D fate

7 I met them .... I didn't know they were going to be there.
   A by luck   B with luck   C by chance   D by fate

8 It was .... that I got the job. I just happened to be in the right place at the right time.
   A fluke   B luck   C fortune   D chance

9 Someone told me he was dishonest. .... , I hadn't given him any money.
   A With luck   B By chance   C Fortunately   D By luck

10 .... ! You deserved to win.
   A Unfair luck   B Nasty luck   C Hard luck   D Bad fortune

11 We had planned to spend the summer in Greece, but .... had obviously decided otherwise.
   A destination   B fortune   C chance   D fate

31.2 *The word in capitals at the end of each of the following sentences can be used to form a word that fits suitably in the blank space. Fill each blank in this way.*

   EXAMPLE We had an interesting *discussion* about football.   DISCUSS

1 I did a very stupid thing, but .... nobody saw me.   LUCK

2 Having our passports stolen was a rather .... start to the holiday.   FORTUNE

3 I'm .... to have such good friends.   LUCK

4 I'd love to see you next week, but .... , it won't be possible.   FORTUNE

5 She must be one of the .... people I know. That's the fourth time her
   flat has been burgled this month.   LUCK

6 Stop complaining! There are many children much less .... than yourself. FORTUNE

31.3 *Finish each of the following sentences in such a way that it means exactly the same as the sentence printed before it.*

> EXAMPLE   Who owns that car?
>
> ANSWER   *Who does that car belong to?* ....

1 I met some old friends by chance in the pub.
   I bumped ....

2 Their party is on the same date as another one I've been invited to.
   Their party coincides ....

3 By chance I was there when she revealed the truth.
   I happened ....

4 If I'm lucky, I'll get a job as soon as I get there.
   With a ....

5 Guess who I met by chance on my way here?
   Guess who I ran ....

6 Fortunately, the boat hadn't left.
   By a stroke ....

7 If nothing unfortunate happens, I'll see you next week.
   All being ....

Unit 32 New/Old

1 **brand-new**
completely new and unused

It looks so clean because it's brand-new.

2 **up to date**
(spelt with hyphens before a
noun)
a modern; the newest of its type

The factory uses the most up-to-date machinery available.

b including or having the most
recent information

*It's not a very up-to-date dictionary./I read a newspaper
every day, so as to keep up to date on what's happening
in the world./I'm up to date with my work. (= I've done
everything I should by now.)*

3 **the latest**
the most modern or most recent

*It's a very modern office, with all the latest technology./I
listen to this programme because they play all the latest
records.*

4 **to update** (sth)
to make something more modern
or up to date

They're updating the office equipment at the moment.

5 **valid**
(of a ticket or document etc.) able
to be used legally

*My passport is valid until the end of the year./I'm afraid
your ticket is not valid on this particular train.*

6 **to run out**
to be no longer valid

*My passport runs out next month, so I'll have to get a new
one.*

7 **to expire**
to run out (of a period of time);
to come to an end

*The Prime Minister's term of office expires next month./My
visa expires next week.*

8 **to renew** (sth)
to replace something old or no
longer valid with something new
or valid

*I've applied to have my visa renewed because I want to
stay here longer./It's about time I had the tyres on my car
renewed.*

9 **to repair** (sth)
to put something which has
broken or is not working properly
into good condition again

*I can't repair the car because I don't know what's wrong
with it.*

10 **to mend** (sth)
to repair

I tried to mend the clock myself and now it's even worse.

11 **to fix** (sth)
to repair

*If you can't fix the car yourself, you'll have to get a
professional to do it.*

12 **to decorate** (sth)
to paint or put up wallpaper etc. on the walls, ceilings etc. of a house

We're going to decorate the house because we don't like the colours.

13 **to do** (sth) **up**
to repair or redecorate(an old building, car etc.)

The house was rather run-down when they bought it but they've done it up and now it's very nice./One of his hobbies is doing up old motorbikes.

14 **to renovate** (sth)
to put (a building, machine etc.) back into good condition by repairing

They'll have to renovate the building because it's in terrible condition./He renovates old farm machinery, which he then sells.

15 **to refurbish** (sth)
to decorate or change the interior (of a building etc.)

The office had to close while it was being refurbished.

Part 2

1 **old-fashioned**
not modern

That style of clothes is old-fashioned now./He's got some very old-fashioned attitudes.

2 **second-hand**
previously owned by someone else; not new

He bought a second-hand car which had had two previous owners.

3 **out of date**
(spelt with hyphens before a noun) old-fashioned; no longer valid or up to date

The equipment needs replacing because it's out of date./ I'm afraid I've got nothing to read except a rather out-of-date copy of The Economist./My licence is out of date – I'd better get a new one.

4 **outdated**
out of date (especially of ideas etc.)

Her teaching methods are rather outdated./He's got some outdated ideas on women and society.

5 **dated**
no longer fashionable or modern

I used to love his music but now it just sounds dated.

6 **antiquated**
very old-fashioned; no longer relevant to the present

That kind of machine looks antiquated now, although it was modern twenty years ago./Many people consider the Royal Family to be an antiquated tradition.

7 **ancient**
extremely old; from or of the distant past

The town is hundreds of years old and has many ancient buildings./She's a professor of ancient history.

8 **an antique**
a very old and valuable object

Be careful with that table – it's an antique.

9 **run-down**
old and in bad condition
(especially of a building or place)

The house is run-down because nobody has looked after it./They live in a rather run-down part of town.

10 **dilapidated**
very run-down; falling to pieces

The house was dilapidated when they bought it, but they've spent a lot of money to make it look nice.

Unit 32 Exercises

32.1 *Choose the word or phrase (A, B, C or D) which best completes each sentence.*

1 A lot of houses in this area are .... because nobody has bothered to look after them.
  A second-hand   B antique   C dilapidated   D out of date

2 My contract .... at the end of the year, so I don't know what I'll do after that.
  A expires   B runs down   C invalidates   D completes

3 I'm not going to take the car to a garage because I think I can .... it myself.
  A renew   B do up   C repair   D renovate

4 It was a very fashionable film years ago, but it looks .... now.
  A outdated   B dilapidated   C dated   D antique

5 The shop is being .... The whole interior is being changed.
  A refurbished   B repaired   C fixed   D mended

6 On the computer system at work, information is .... every hour.
  A renewed   B renovated   C updated   D done up

7 This train ticket is .... until the end of the month.
  A updated   B worthy   C valid   D validated

8 The insurance on the car runs out next week. I'd better ....
  A update it   B renovate it   C renew it   D run it in

9 This is a .... neighbourhood. Most of the buildings are in bad condition.
  A damaged   B dated   C run-down   D run-out

10 My hi-fi seems rather .... now. Well, I suppose it is over ten years old.
  A antiquated   B antique   C expired   D run-down

11 I couldn't afford a new guitar so I bought a(n) .... one.
  A old-fashioned   B outdated   C second-hand   D antiquated

12 We had to .... the room because the wallpaper was in terrible condition.
  A renovate   B renew   C decorate   D mend

13 Is this information .... ? Does it include the most recent changes?
  A modern   B up to date   C brand-new   D renewed

14 There's no need to throw that shirt away. It can easily be ....
  A done up   B renewed   C mended   D cured

15 They took us to see an .... monument which was built almost a thousand years ago.
  A outdated   B antique   C antiquated   D ancient

16 My passport is .... so I can't use it any longer.
  A ancient   B outdated   C out of date   D dated

17 I read a newspaper every day because I like to know the .... news.
   A last B ultimate C latest D newest

18 They bought an old house, ... , and then sold it.
   A redid it B did it in C did it up D overdid it

19 My grandmother's house is full of valuable ....
   A ancients B antiquities C antiques D antiquarians

20 'Gramophone' is an .... word for 'record player'.
   A antique B old-fashioned C outdated D ancient

21 You'll never .... that typewriter. Can't you see it's beyond repair?
   A renew B update C renovate D fix

22 Dad's just bought a(n) .... car.
   A updated B brand-new C newest D latest

23 The house has just been .... , so I'm sure you'll agree it's a very fair price.
   A renovated B renewed C done over D updated

24 Her contract .... in two months, so she's looking for another job.
   A runs down B runs out C goes out D goes away

25 His views on education are somewhat ....
   A expired B run-down C outdated D ancient

Unit 33 Rich/Poor

Part 1

1 **rich**
having a lot of money or
possessions etc.

He doesn't have to worry about money because his family is rich.

2 **wealthy**
rich

He doesn't have to work because he comes from a wealthy family.

3 **wealth**
(the possession of) a large amount
of money etc.

A lot of his wealth came from clever investment.

4 **well-off**
rich enough to be able to do most
of the things that you would like
to do

They must be well-off – they get a new car every year./I don't enjoy my new job as much as my old one, but I'm much better off.

5 **comfortable**
fairly well-off; not poor

They haven't got an enormous amount of money but they're relatively comfortable.

6 **affluent**
rich and with a high standard of
living

They lead a very affluent lifestyle./The Government's always telling us we live in an affluent society, but personally I have no experience of it.

7 **to be able to afford** (sth/*to do*
sth)
to have enough money to buy or
do something

I can't afford it – it's way beyond my price range./How much can you afford to spend?

8 **to be rolling in money/it**
(*colloquial*) to be very rich

She can buy anything she wants – she's rolling in money./ They must be absolutely rolling in it to live in a house like that.

9 **a fortune**
a large amount of money

She started with very little but she's made a fortune over the years./He won a fortune on the football pools./What an incredible necklace – it must be worth a fortune.

10 **luxury**
very great comfort, as made
possible by wealth

She now lives a life of luxury, somewhere in the Caribbean./Compared with some hotels I've stayed in, this is luxury./It's her ambition to live in luxury.

11 **a luxury**
something which is considered to
be unnecessary or which you do
not often have or do, but which
provides great pleasure

Eating out in restaurants is a bit of a luxury for us./Most people nowadays regard television as a necessity rather than a luxury./It would be nice to be able to afford a few luxuries.

12 **luxurious**
very comfortable and expensive

They live in a luxurious apartment.

13 **a millionaire**
an extremely rich person;
(*literally*) a person who has a
million pounds or dollars

He started with nothing and he's a millionaire now.

14 **flash**
(*colloquial*) attractive and
expensive looking

Have you seen her flash new car?

Part 2

1 **poor**
having little or no wealth or
possessions

They were too poor to afford decent clothes./He's rich now, but he's never forgotten that he came from a poor family.

2 **poverty**
the state of being very poor

There's a lot of poverty in that country./Nobody wants to live in poverty.

3 **broke**
(*colloquial*) having no money
(often only temporarily)

I can't go out tonight – I'm broke.

4 **hard up**
not having enough money to buy
the things that you need

We're all going to be rather hard up for a while, until Dad manages to find a new job.

5 **short (of money)**
fairly hard up

I'm short of money myself at the moment, so I'm afraid I can't lend you any.

6 **skint**
(*colloquial*) completely without
money

Could you lend me some money? I'm skint.

7 **tight**
(of money) in short supply

I was wondering if you could wait a bit longer for that money I owe you. You see, money's a bit tight at the moment.

8 **hardship**
difficulties in life, often related to
poverty; lack of basic necessities

There's a lot of hardship in areas with high unemployment.

9 **to owe** (s.o. sth)
to have an obligation to pay

Don't forget that you owe me £10./I still owe them £300 for that decorating they did.

10 **a debt**
money that you owe

They've got a huge debt with the bank./He always pays his debts promptly.

11 **to be in debt** (*to* s.o.)
to be in the position of owing
money

I never borrow money because I hate being in debt to anyone./She suddenly found herself heavily in debt.

Unit 33 Exercises

33.1 *Choose the word or phrase (A, B, C or D) which best completes each sentence.*

1 I wouldn't say that I was rich, but I'm ....
A affluent   B wealthy   C flash   D comfortable

2 I haven't got any money at all. I'm completely ....
A broken   B hard up   C short   D broke

3 Could you lend me some money? I'm a bit .... at the moment.
A hard up   B tight   C indebted   D down-and-out

4 They live .... in a huge villa in France.
A in luxury   B with luxury   C in wealth   D with fortune

5 It's a really .... area. Everyone's got expensive houses and cars there.
A affluent   B comfortable   C luxurious   D fortunate

6 I wouldn't say they were rich, but they're certainly ....
A wealthy   B well-earned   C well-off   D well-kept

7 Money's very .... this month, so we can't afford to go out.
A broke   B tight   C hard   D hard up

8 I mustn't borrow any more money – I'm already badly ....
A in deed   B on loan   C in debt   D in doubt

9 I like your new suit – very .... !
A rich   B well-off   C flash   D affluent

10 She was so .... that she was forced to steal.
A tight   B poorly   C poor   D broken

11 He may have a nice house, a nice car and be able to afford to go on nice holidays, but you couldn't say he was ....
A well-off   B rich   C rolling   D comfortable

12 I'm .... already, and it's another two weeks until pay-day.
A poor   B tight   C hard   D skint

13 I don't have to get up until ten o'clock tomorrow – what a ....!
A luxury   B wealth   C fortune   D comfort

14 .... does not always bring happiness.
A Riches   B Health   C Abundance   D Wealth

33.2 *The word in capitals at the end of each of the following sentences can be used to form a word that fits suitably in the blank space. Fill each blank in this way.*

EXAMPLE We had an interesting *discussion* about football.   DISCUSS

1 I've known .... all my life. There have been times when I couldn't even afford a loaf of bread.   HARD

2 He became a .... at the age of twenty-five.   MILLION

3 She's got very .... parents.   WEALTH

149

4 Even in a supposedly rich country like Britain, there are still thousands of people living in ....   POOR

5 This car is really ....   LUXURY

33.3 *Fill each of the blanks with one suitable word.*

1 Have you seen her enormous diamond ring? It must have cost a .... !

2 I'm so hard up at the moment that I can't even .... to buy you a drink.

3 If you take that job, you'll be .... -off than you are now, because the salary's lower.

4 I lent him £20 last month which he still .... me.

5 He's got so many .... from all the money he's borrowed that I don't know how he'll ever be able to pay them all off.

6 That's the fifth new car they've bought this month. They must be .... in money!

7 Could I borrow £5 to pay the bill? I'm a bit .... of money at the moment.

Unit 34 Suitable/Convenient

1 **suitable** (*for* s.o./sth)
right or acceptable for a particular
person, purpose or occasion etc.

*I'm looking for a suitable present to get my wife for her
birthday./He's not suitable for this job – he's too quiet./
The flat has three large bedrooms and would be suitable
for a family.*

2 **unsuitable**
not suitable

*They rejected the candidate because he was totally
unsuitable.*

3 **to suit** (s.o.)
a to be acceptable or satisfactory
for someone

*I can come at any time that suits you./Does this room suit
you or would you prefer something bigger?*

b to look good on someone; to
make someone look attractive

Your new hairstyle suits you./That colour doesn't suit him.

4 **to be suited** (*to* s.o./sth)
to have the right qualities or be of
the right type for a particular
purpose or person

*I don't think he's really suited to being a salesman./Nick
and his new girlfriend seem really well suited, don't you
agree?*

5 **right** (*for* s.o./sth)
best in view of the circumstances

*Are you sure you're making the right decision?/She's the
right person for the job./They shouldn't have got married
– he's not right for her.*

6 **convenient**
a (*for* s.o.)
suiting someone's plans or a
particular purpose, without
causing any problems

*Can we arrange a meeting for tomorrow? Would two
o'clock be convenient?/I'm afraid this isn't a very
convenient place to talk./I'll come back at a time that's
more convenient for you.*

b (*for* sth)
(in a place which is) useful in
saving you time and effort

*The flat is convenient for the shops and the underground
station./Having a bus stop outside our house is very
convenient.*

7 **inconvenient**
not convenient

*They came at an inconvenient time – we were in the
middle of eating.*

8 **appropriate**
right or suitable for the particular
circumstances

*I don't think jeans would be appropriate at this type of
party.*

9 **inappropriate**
not appropriate

*I realised that what I was wearing was completely
inappropriate for such a formal occasion.*

10 **fit** (*for* s.o./sth)
good enough or suitable enough
for a particular person, purpose or
thing etc.

*These houses aren't fit to be lived in./The food we received
in prison wasn't fit for an animal, let alone a human
being.*

11 **unfit**
not fit

This meat is unfit for human consumption.

12 **to fit** (s.o.) to be the correct size and shape etc.	*These trousers don't fit (me) – they're too tight.*
13 **to fit in** to be suitable for a particular situation or group of people etc.	*She immediately fitted in because she had the same sense of humour as the rest of the staff.*
14 **to match** (sth) to be of a suitable colour or design etc. for use with something else	*His tie doesn't match his shirt./We're looking for some curtains to match the wallpaper.*
15 **to clash** (*with* sth) to be of a completely unsuitable colour or design for use with something else; not to match	*Her blouse clashes with her skirt.*
16 **in bad taste** unsuitable, rude or not funny in view of the circumstances	*His jokes about the plane crash were in bad taste.*

Unit 34 Exercises

34.1 *Choose the word or phrase (A, B, C or D) which best completes each sentence.*

1 He changed jobs because he decided that being a computer programmer wasn't .... for him.
  A fit   B right   C convenient   D suited

2 He isn't .... such a responsible job. He's hopeless at making decisions.
  A fit for   B convenient for   C fitted in   D suited

3 I turned down the job because it was .... It wasn't what I was looking for.
  A unsuitable   B unfit   C inappropriate   D unsuited

4 I left London because I wasn't .... the hectic lifestyle.
  A suited for   B convenient for   C suitable for   D suited to

5 I once knew a man called Mr Good – a rather .... name considering he was sent to prison for shoplifting!
  A unfit   B inappropriate   C inconvenient   D unsuited

6 These flats are clearly .... for people to live in – they should be pulled down immediately.
  A unfit   B inappropriate   C inconvenient   D unsuited

7 She hasn't made many friends at university – she doesn't really seem to ....
  A suit   B match   C fit in   D take to

8 I don't think his speech was really .... for a wedding – it was too depressing.
  A fit   B convenient   C appropriate   D suited

34.2 *Fill each of the blanks with one suitable word.*

1 If Tuesday doesn't .... you, we could meet on Wednesday instead.

2 She spent a long time looking for a sofa that would .... the carpets.

3 Would it be more .... you if I came to your house, instead of you to mine?

4 You can't put the table in that corner because it won't .... – it's too big.

5 He called at a very .... time – we were right in the middle of dinner.

6 Making jokes at grandad's funeral was in very ....

7 You look great in that dress, it really .... you!

8 Where I'm living is .... work because I don't have to travel far.

9 I saw a few flats but none of them were .... for me. They were all too small.

10 You can't possibly wear those trousers. They .... with your jacket.

Unit 35 Usual/Unusual/Strange

Part 1

1 **usual**
happening, used, done etc. most often

I sat in my usual seat./Is it usual to have so much rain at this time of year?/It's usual for people to send cards at Christmas.

2 **common**
happening or found often or in many places

That's a common mistake so don't worry about it./The commonest surname in Britain is probably Smith./It's now quite common in Britain for couples to live together before getting married.

3 **normal**
in accordance with what people expect or with what is usual; not strange

After yesterday's accident on the motorway, traffic is now back to normal./It's been a normal day – nothing unusual has happened./Is it normal for the train to be late?

4 **ordinary**
not unusual or special

I come from an ordinary town – there's nothing particularly interesting about it.

5 **everyday**
common and ordinary (of events that happen as part of normal life)

She gets upset about everyday problems./Train cancellations and delays seem to have become an everyday occurence.

6 **average**
a normal (statistically) for a particular group of people or things

The average age in my class is twenty-one.

b ordinary; neither very good nor very bad

'What was the meal like?' – 'Average – I've had better.'

7 **on average**
usually or generally (statistically)

On average I work about forty hours a week.

8 **standard**
of the usual type

It's standard procedure for most companies to ask prospective employees for references.

9 **conventional**
following the usual and accepted ways of behaviour (within a particular society)

It's conventional to wear formal clothes at weddings.

10 **typical** (*of* s.o./sth)
a showing the most usual qualities of a particular type of person or thing (and therefore a very good example of that type)

This is a typical Spanish meal./This style of architecture is typical of the region.

b showing the usual behaviour, exactly as you would expect (used to complain about someone or something)

It's typical of him to turn up late./'It's raining again' – 'Typical!'

154

11 **characteristic** (*of* s.o./sth)
typical of a person or thing's
usual character or behaviour

The elephant let out its characteristic cry./Such generosity is characteristic of him.

12 **representative** (*of* s.o./sth)
being a typical example of a
particular group (and therefore
showing what the rest of the
group is like)

I hope you don't think that his opinions are representative of all English people.

Part 2

1 **unusual**
   a not usual or common

It's unusual for him to lose his temper./That's an unusual name. It's not English, is it?

   b interesting, because of being
   different from other things of the
   same type

She's got an unusual face, quite beautiful in fact./It's certainly an unusual building, but I'm not sure if I like it or not.

2 **rare**
very unusual or uncommon

It's rare to see that kind of old car these days./The law aims to protect rare or endangered species.

3 **scarce**
not common, because of being
difficult to find or in short supply

At this time of year some vegetables are scarce.

4 **special**
unusual and important; not of the
ordinary type

We had an expensive meal on my birthday, as it was a special occasion./'What are you doing this weekend?' – 'Nothing special.'

5 **extraordinary**
very unusual, surprising or special

By an extraordinary coincidence my husband, mother, and brother all share the same birthday./My mother is an extraordinary woman.

6 **remarkable**
very unusual, exceptional and
noticeable

His success is a remarkable achievement considering the problems he has had.

7 **unique**
   a being the only one of its type

This Louis XV chair is unique.

   b very unusual and special

Spending six months in India was a unique experience.

8 **to be unique to** (s.o./sth)
to be found only in one particular
person, thing, place etc.

The bouto river dolphin is unique to the Amazon./This style of painting is unique to Van Gogh.

9 **strange**
difficult to explain or understand;
unusual

It's strange that she hasn't phoned me for so long – she usually phones every week./He has some very strange ideas.

10 **odd**
strange or unusual; different from what you would expect

How odd that nobody is here to meet us./Her behaviour has been rather odd recently.

11 **peculiar**
strange (sometimes in an unpleasant way)

That's peculiar – I had it a minute ago and now I can't find it./They have some peculiar habits./This soup tastes rather peculiar – do you think it's all right?

12 **to be peculiar to** (s.o./sth)
to be unique to a particular person, thing, place etc.

Flamenco dancing is peculiar to Spain.

13 **curious**
strange, interesting and possibly mysterious

It's a curious fact that the richer he gets, the more miserable he becomes.

14 **funny**
slightly strange or surprising

He's got some funny ideas, which don't make any sense to me.

15 **unreal**
(of an experience) very strange; seeming to belong in a dream

I've had so much bad news recently that it's unreal.

16 **weird**
(*colloquial*) very strange and often mysterious; difficult to accept as normal

That's weird – I remember putting the letter in this drawer, but it's not here now./She's got some very weird ideas./He's really weird – you never know what he's going to do.

17 **unconventional**
not conventional

Some people stare at him because of his unconventional way of dressing.

18 **eccentric**
(of a person) behaving in a way which other people consider to be strange and slightly amusing

He's got some very eccentric habits, and it's quite common for him to go to work without any shoes on.

19 **uncharacteristic**
not characteristic

It's uncharacteristic of her to use bad language.

Unit 35 Exercises

35.1 *Choose the word or phrase (A, B, C or D) which best completes each sentence.*

1 There's a(n) .... smell in here. What on earth is it?
A odd   B rare   C special   D scarce

2 It's .... that he never mentioned our argument; I wonder why he didn't.
A special   B rare   C curious   D eccentric

3 The programme examines what .... people feel about fashion.
A average   B typical   C standard   D ordinary

4 It's .... for people to get depressed if they're out of work.
   A normal   B everyday   C representative   D typical

5 He deals with the .... matters in the office; his boss deals with the important ones.
   A everyday   B average   C usual   D standard

6 Opportunities as good as that are ....
   A scarce   B peculiar   C weird   D unconventional

7 It's .... of her to refuse to admit that she's wrong; she's very stubborn.
   A characteristic   B ordinary   C average   D representative

8 It's .... for me to get so upset about such a small problem; I normally don't let such things worry me.
   A eccentric   B unusual   C remarkable   D scarce

9 I thought it was going to be a brilliant show because of the reviews, but it was only ....
   A normal   B common   C average   D usual

10 What a(n) .... thing to say! What gave you that idea?
   A unique   B peculiar   C unreal   D scarce

11 He's not crazy, he's just a bit .... , that's all.
   A uncharacteristic   B unreal   C eccentric   D unique

12 Because she doesn't behave in a very .... way, people think that she's rather strange.
   A usual   B conventional   C standard   D average

13 The .... temperature for August was 25°C
   A common   B average   C typical   D representative

14 Is it .... for people to behave like that in this country?
   A representative   B usual   C average   D everyday

15 There were some very .... people at that party last night. They scared me a bit, actually.
   A unreal   B remarkable   C weird   D uncharacteristic

16 That's .... The bus is usually on time, so I've no idea why it's late today.
   A strange   B rare   C scarce   D special

17 John took us all out for a meal as a(n) .... treat.
   A unique   B special   C uncharacteristic   D scarce

18 He's got into trouble at work on several occasions because of his .... way of dealing with clients.
   A unconventional   B rare   C uncharacteristic   D remarkable

19 That's .... – I'm sure I left my watch on the table but it doesn't seem to be there any more.
   A funny   B unique   C rare   D scarce

20 Smoking is the most .... cause of lung cancer.
   A ordinary   B average   C normal   D common

21 We were given the .... opportunity of seeing inside Buckingham Palace.
   A peculiar   B unique   C scarce   D odd

22 The car costs £12,095 for the .... model, and £14,250 for the de luxe version.
   A average   B standard   C common   D typical

23 The stamp is so .... that there are only thought to be three of them in the whole world.
   A weird B rare C strange D odd

35.2 *Fill each of the blanks with one suitable word.*

1 It's typical .... him to forget my birthday!

2 Her accent is peculiar .... the North-East.

3 .... average I go out about three evenings a week.

4 These hooligans are by no means representative .... the majority of football fans.

5 This particular problem of pronunciation is unique .... German speakers.

35.3 *The word in capitals at the end of each of the following sentences can be used to form a word that fits suitably in the blank space. Fill each blank in this way.*

   EXAMPLE We had an interesting *discussion* about football.   DISCUSS

1 It's .... of him to lose his temper like that – he's usually very calm.   CHARACTER

2 Considering the amount of work there was, it's .... that you've managed
  to finish it all so quickly.   REMARK

3 So many things have been going wrong recently that it's .... – it seems
  like a nightmare.   REAL

4 Snow in August ! How .... !   ORDINARY

5 I met some tourists who asked me where they could find a .... English pub.   TYPE

Section D
Thought, Knowledge and Ability

Units 36-43

Unit 36 Ability

1 **to be good** (*at* sth/*at doing* sth)
to be able to do something well

He's good at crosswords./She's very good at telling jokes.

2 **to be not very good** (*at* sth/*at doing* sth)
to be unable to do something well

I'm not very good at expressing myself.

3 **to be no good** (*at* sth/*at doing* sth)
to be completely unable to do something well; to do something very badly

I'm no good at sport.

4 **to be hopeless** (*at* sth/*at doing* sth)
to be no good at something

I'm hopeless at spelling.

5 **to be capable** (*of* sth/*of doing* sth)
a to have the ability or potential ability to do something

She's capable of being very successful./He's not capable of looking after himself.

b to be able to do something if required

This knife is capable of cutting anything you want it to cut./This car is capable of a top speed of 200 m.p.h.

6 **to be/feel up to** (sth/*doing* sth)
(usually used in negative statements or questions) to be or feel well enough or capable enough (physically or mentally) to do something

I don't feel up to going out tonight – I'm too tired./Do you think she's up to the job?/I don't think my car is really up to driving on this kind of road.

7 **to come naturally**
to be something that you are able to do easily, without effort

Languages seem to come naturally to her.

8 **talent**
natural ability to do something well (especially creative things)

To be a good actor, hard work is not enough – you must have talent.

9 **skill**
an ability produced by training

It takes a lot of skill to be a surgeon.

10 **a gift** (*for* sth/*for doing* sth)
natural ability; talent

He has a gift for music./She has a wonderful gift for telling stories.

11 **a flair** (*for* sth/*for doing* sth)
natural ability to do something well and in an interesting way

He has a flair for cooking and invents some wonderful new recipes.

12 **a knack** (*of doing* sth)
a special ability that cannot be
explained

He has a knack of being in the right place at the right time.

13 **to enable** (s.o. *to do* sth)
to make it possible for someone to
do something

The bank loan enabled him to start his own company.

Unit 36 Exercises

36.1 *Fill each of the blanks with one suitable word.*

1 This game isn't simply a question of luck, you also need ....

2 He has a .... languages and has always been able to learn them very quickly.

3 How's your stomach now? Do you feel .... having something to eat?

4 Although he has plenty of .... , he doesn't have the ambition to be a professional musician.

5 I don't know why, but I seem to have a .... of saying the wrong thing.

6 I don't need anyone's help. I'm .... of doing it myself.

7 She has a .... organising parties, and always provides something unusual.

36.2 *For each of the sentences below, write a new sentence as similar as possible in meaning to the original sentence, but using the word given. This word must not be altered in any way.*

EXAMPLE   It's no use arguing: I've made up my mind.
          point

ANSWER   *There's no point in arguing; I've made up my mind.*

1 She won't be able to understand something as difficult as that.
capable

....

2 Card games are not my speciality, although I can play a bit.
good

....

3 Because of good advice, I was able to make the right decision.
enabled

....

4 I've tried, but I simply can't cook at all.
good

....

5 He finds it impossible to make decisions.
hopeless

....

6 I found swimming easy.
naturally

....

7 She can explain things well.
good

....

Unit 37 Anticipate/Predict

Part 1

1 **to anticipate** (sth/*doing* sth/ *that* ...)
to feel that something will happen

Are you anticipating a large crowd tonight?/I don't anticipate being here for very long./Do you anticipate any problems?/I didn't anticipate that the journey would take so long.

2 **in anticipation of**
having anticipated

I had made sure of my facts in anticipation of an argument.

3 **to foresee** (sth)
to see or know in advance that something is going to happen

I don't foresee any problems – I'm sure everything will be all right.

4 **unforeseen**
not seen in advance; unexpected

Unless anything unforeseen happens, I'll see you on Friday.

5 **the foreseeable future**
as much of the future as you can see

I'm going to stay here for the foreseeable future.

6 **to predict** (sth/*that* ...)
to make a statement about what will happen in the future

It's impossible to predict the result of the next election./ She predicted that I would be married with two children within five years.

7 **predictable**
possible to predict

The film had a rather predictable ending – I'd guessed halfway through who the murderer was.

8 **unpredictable**
impossible to predict

The weather tends to be somewhat unpredictable at this time of year.

9 **a prediction**
a statement about what will happen in the future

All the predictions in my horoscope indicate that I'm going to have a good month.

10 **to forecast** (sth)
to make a prediction (based on expert knowledge)

The Stock Exchange is forecasting another rise in interest rates./Rain is forecast for this afternoon.

11 **a forecast**
a prediction based on expert knowledge

Do you know what the weather forecast is for today?/The economic forecast for the next six months is very good.

12 **to imagine** (sth/*doing* sth)
to form a mental image or picture of something

Can you imagine his face when I told him the news?/I can imagine how you felt. It must have been awful./Imagine not having to go to work tomorrow! Wouldn't it be wonderful?/I can't imagine myself working here much longer.

13 **to come up**
to happen or appear unexpectedly

Unless something comes up, I'll see you tomorrow./It came up in conversation that we both knew the same people.

163

14 **to crop up**
to come up (often something
unpleasant)

I'm afraid I can't meet you tonight – something's cropped up at work.

15 **to turn up**
to come up (often something
good)

I don't know what I'm going to do next year, but I'm sure something will turn up.

16 **an expectation**
a strong hope and belief about
what something will be like;
something that you anticipate or
regard as probable

I had high expectations of the film but it wasn't very good./The world champion has, against all expectations, lost.

17 **to live up to** (sth)
to be as good as or equal to (your
expectations etc.)

The hotel didn't really live up to our expectations.

18 **prospect** (*of* sth/*of doing* sth)
expectation; mental picture of the
future; chance or possibility

I don't fancy the prospect of living here all my life./The prospect of a holiday cheered her up immensely./There isn't much prospect of her changing her mind.

19 **prospects**
chances for future success

They left the country because they felt that their prospects were better abroad.

20 **the outlook**
the probable or expected future
situation (often as seen by an
expert)

According to economists the outlook is good.

21 **potential**
possible, but not yet actual

Many people feel that the Government's policy is a potential disaster.

22 **potentially**

I think this is a potentially good idea, which might well succeed.

23 **potential**
possible future ability (to do
something well or succeed)

She has the potential to be a very good teacher./She's got definite management potential./Your idea has potential.

24 **scope** (*for* sth/*for doing* sth)
opportunity (to think or act freely)

I took the job because there was scope for introducing my own ideas./I wish there was more scope for creativity in my job.

Part 2

1 **inevitable**
certain to happen; unable to be
prevented

He never looked after himself so it was inevitable that one day he would be seriously ill.

2 **a foregone conclusion**
a completely predictable result

His exam result was a foregone conclusion – he was obviously going to pass.

3 **to be liable** (*to do* sth)
to be likely to do something

My car is very old and it's liable to break down at any time.

4 **to run the risk** (*of* sth/*of doing* sth)
to take the chance (of something dangerous or unpleasant happening)

If you expect too much, you run the risk of disappointment./Anyone who smokes runs the risk of getting cancer.

5 **touch and go**
not certain; difficult to predict (whether something will or will not happen)

During his first few days in hospital, it was touch and go whether he would survive.

6 **in doubt**
with an uncertain future

The game is in doubt because of the weather./His job is in doubt because the company's doing badly.

7 **the odds**
the probability (of something happening)

I'm not sure, but the odds are that you'll find what you want in that shop.

8 **to gamble** (*on doing* sth)
to take a risk in expectation of success etc.

We haven't booked in advance – we're gambling on getting tickets when we arrive.

9 **there's no telling/knowing**
it is impossible to predict

There's no telling what he'll say./There's no knowing what might happen.

10 **it remains to be seen**
it will only be known in the future

Everything looks good at the moment but it remains to be seen what will happen.

Unit 37 Exercises

37.1 *Choose the word or phrase (A, B, C or D) which best completes each sentence.*

1 The plane was late taking off, due to .... mechanical problems.
A inevitable B unforeseen C unimagined D unpredictable

2 The ending of the joke was so .... that no one laughed.
A predictable B potential C foreseen D anticipated

3 The job has no ....
A perspective B outlook C prospects D expectations

4 He's .... on getting another job straightaway.
A anticipating B risking C expecting D gambling

5 If he carries on like that, he's running the .... of a heart attack.
A odds B risk C gamble D liability

6 There's not much .... for progression in this job.
A prospect   B outlook   C expectation   D scope

7 I've got to work late tonight – something has ....
A come out   B turned out   C come up   D turned off

8 There's not much .... of him finding a cheap hotel in such an expensive city.
A potential   B prospect   C outlook   D scope

9 She's got the .... to do well.
A potential   B prospect   C outlook   D scope

10 I don't think that the situation will change in the .... future.
A known   B predictable   C foreseen   D foreseeable

11 The weather .... said it was going to rain today.
A prediction   B prospect   C forecast   D scope

12 I can't imagine .... anywhere except London.
A living   B to live   C live   D that I live

13 The newspapers are .... that there will be a general election in two months.
A turning up   B forecasting   C imagining   D telling

14 My .... was right. The result of the game was exactly what I said it would be.
A anticipation   B prospect   C prediction   D outlook

15 For me, the film didn't .... all the enthusiastic publicity it received.
A come up   B live up   C turn up to   D live up to

16 Don't worry about not finding a job yet. I'm sure something will turn .... soon.
A up   B out   C about   D in

17 I .... that the score would be 2-0 but I was wrong.
A told   B predicted   C looked out   D cropped up

18 He was late so often that it was .... that he would lose his job eventually.
A forecast   B inevitable   C potential   D anticipated

19 I didn't .... that such a simple matter could become as complicated as it has.
A foresee   B gamble   C forecast   D tell

37.2 *The word in capitals at the end of each of the following sentences can be used to form a word that fits suitably in the blank space. Fill each blank in this way.*

EXAMPLE We had an interesting *discussion* about football.   DISCUSS

1 I left early in .... of heavy traffic.   ANTICIPATE

2 She's very .... – you never know whether she's going to
be in a good mood or in a bad mood.   PREDICT

3 Her latest book didn't really live up to my ....   EXPECT

4 Sales forecasts indicate a poor .... for the clothing industry.   LOOK

5 There's no .... how he will react.   KNOW

37.3 *For each of the sentences below, write a new sentence as similar as possible in meaning to the original sentence, but using the word given. This word must not be altered in any way.*

EXAMPLE   It's no use arguing: I've made up my mind.
point

ANSWER   *There's no point in arguing; I've made up my mind.*
....

1 I'll have to wait before I know whether he'll keep his promise or not.
remains

....

2 I'm afraid I'll be a bit late because something unexpected has happened.
cropped

....

3 There was never any doubt about what the result would be.
conclusion

....

4 What you're doing might be dangerous.
potentially

....

5 It's impossible to predict how long it will take to do this.
telling

....

6 I shouldn't think that anything will go wrong.
odds

....

7 The party might not happen, because she's ill.
doubt

....

8 He'll probably get here late; he usually does.
liable

....

9 The profit that might be made is enormous.
potential

....

10 It's not certain whether I'll be able to pay the bills this month.
touch

....

11 I don't think I'll see him for some time.
anticipate

....

Unit 38 Concentrate/Interrupt

Part 1

1 **to concentrate** (*on* sth/*on doing* sth)
to give all your attention to something

He doesn't go out much because he wants to concentrate on his work./I'm concentrating on making as much money as possible.

Note: **to be concentrated in** = to be all together in one place

The industry is concentrated in one part of the country.

2 **concentration**
the ability to concentrate

Most people lose concentration if they work for too long.

3 **to focus** (*on* sth)
to concentrate on one particular part of something

The play focuses on the story of two of the characters.

4 **to get down to** (sth)
to start doing something, especially something which requires concentration or attention

I'll have to get down to some work soon – I haven't done any for ages./Right, let's get down to business, shall we?

5 **to be engrossed** (*in* sth)
to have your interest and attention completely held by something, and not to be aware of anything else

I didn't hear you arrive because I was engrossed in a book.

6 **to be preoccupied** (*with* sth)
not to be able to concentrate because of thinking about something else

He can't concentrate on his job because he's preoccupied with his personal problems./You seem rather preoccupied – are you worried about something?

7 **to leave** (s.o.) **alone**
to allow someone to be alone; not to disturb someone

I should leave him alone, he's busy at the moment.

Part 2

1 **to interrupt** (s.o.)
to stop someone in the middle of doing something

He interrupted me before I'd finished explaining./I'm sorry to interrupt you while you're eating, but I must speak to you.

2 **to disturb** (s.o.)
to interrupt someone's peace, concentration etc.

Don't disturb your father just now – he's working./I hope I didn't disturb you by phoning so late. Were you asleep?

3 **to distract** (s.o.)
to take someone's attention away from what they are doing

The noise outside distracted me while I was trying to work.

4 **to put** (s.o.) **off**
to distract someone; to make it
difficult for someone to
concentrate

Stop talking, you're putting me off. I'm trying to think.

5 **to butt in**
to speak before someone else has
finished what they are saying,
often rudely

I wish you'd stop butting in and let me finish my story.

6 **to intrude** (*on* s.o./sth)
to disturb someone's privacy; to
enter a situation where you are
not wanted

*I hope I'm not intruding on you./Sorry to intrude on your
meeting, but there's an urgent phone call for Mr Shaw./
The questions on this form intrude on my private life.*

7 **to get in the way** (*of* sth)
to make it difficult for someone to
do something (by being an
obstacle)

His social life gets in the way of his studies.

Unit 38 Exercises

38.1 *Choose the word or phrase (A, B, C or D) which best completes each sentence.*

1 I wish you wouldn't keep .... me. Let me finish what I'm saying.
   A intruding   B disturbing   C interrupting   D butting in

2 After a while I was so tired that I couldn't ....
   A be engrossed   B be focused   C concentrate   D be concentrated

3 I think we should .... the most important points.
   A be concentrated on   B be concentrated in   C focus on   D concentrate in

4 I didn't notice the time because I was so .... in my work.
   A concentrated   B engrossed   C focused   D preoccupied

5 Every time I started to say something, he ....
   A distracted   B disturbed   C butted   D butted in

6 Most of the population .... the cities.
   A is concentrated in   B is concentrated on   C concentrates on   D is engrossed in

7 I find it difficult to keep my .... if the television is on while I'm working.
   A concentration   B focus   C preoccupation   D dedication

8 I hope the baby didn't .... you during the night.
   A distract   B disturb   C intrude   D butt in

9 Driving through Rome, I was .... for a second and ended up going into the back of the car
   in front!
   A disturbed   B distracted   C got in the way of   D engrossed

38.2 *For each of the sentences below, write a new sentence as similar as possible in meaning to the original sentence, but using the word given. This word must not be altered in any way.*

> EXAMPLE It's no use arguing: I've made up my mind.
> **point**
>
> ANSWER *There's no point in arguing; I've made up my mind.*

1 If you gave your mind to your work, you might not make so many mistakes.
concentrated

....

2 A lot of things keep stopping me from working.
way

....

3 You'll have to start doing some serious work soon.
get

....

4 I'm trying to concentrate, but all that noise you're making is distracting me.
putting

....

5 I don't like disturbing her when she's busy.
intruding

....

6 Stop disturbing me! Can't you see I'm working?
alone

....

7 His mind is so much on work at the moment that he doesn't have any time for his family.
preoccupied

....

Unit 39 Consider/Change your Mind

1 **to consider** (sth/*doing* sth)
to think carefully about
something; to have as a possible
plan

Before you decide to resign, consider the consequences./
I'm considering resigning but I haven't decided yet.

2 **to take** (sth) **into consideration**
to consider something when
making a decision (because you
think it is important)

They took into consideration the experience of each
candidate before deciding who to offer the job to./They
took the experience of each candidate into consideration
before deciding who to offer the job to.

3 **to take** (sth) **into account**
to take into consideration

Stop worrying about the exam! I'm sure your teacher will
take your illness into account./Stop worrying about the
exam! I'm sure your teacher will take into account your
illness.

4 **to bear** (sth) **in mind**
to consider or remember
something before making a
judgement

If you bear in mind her problems, it's not surprising she's
miserable./You speak English very well, bearing in mind
that you've only been learning it for four months.

5 **to allow for** (sth)
to take particular circumstances
(a problem, someone's weakness
etc.) into consideration

She's not stupid. You just have to allow for the fact that
she has no experience of this kind of situation./Allowing
for the traffic, it'll take about forty minutes to get there.

6 **to make allowances for**
a (s.o.)
to be more tolerant of someone
because they have a particular
problem or difficulty

You've got to make allowances for her. She had a very
unhappy childhood./Don't worry, we all know you're new
to the job and we all make allowances for you.

b (sth)
to allow for

I know he says some stupid things but you have to make
allowances for his age.

7 **to have in mind**
to be considering (a plan or idea);
to intend

'Will you do me a favour?' – 'It depends on what you
have in mind.'/I know I said that I wanted a holiday, but a
weekend at your mother's wasn't exactly what I had in
mind!

8 **to be thinking of** (*doing* sth)
to be considering (a possible plan)

I'm thinking of going away this weekend.

9 **to think** (sth) **over**
to consider carefully before
deciding

It's a big decision – I'll have to think it over.

10 **to weigh up the pros and cons**
to consider the advantages and
disadvantages

I'll have to weigh up the pros and cons before making a
decision.

11 **all things considered**
after considering the advantages
and disadvantages

Even though we had some complaints, all things considered, it was a good holiday.

12 **to be in two minds** (*about* sth)
to be unable to decide (between
two possibilities)

I'm in two minds about whether to change my job.

13 **to change your mind**
to change a decision

I said I was going to leave, but I've changed my mind – I've decided to stay.

14 **to have second thoughts** (*about* sth/*about doing* sth)
to have doubts about a decision;
not to know if your decision was
the right decision

I accepted the offer, but now I'm having second thoughts about it./We had second thoughts about buying the house when we found out how much it cost.

15 **on second thoughts**
having thought about it again (an
expression used when you change
your mind about something)

I had decided to accept the offer, but on second thoughts I don't think I will./I'll have a coffee. No, on second thoughts I'll have an orange juice.

16 **to think twice** (*about* sth/*about doing* sth)
to think very carefully about an
important decision; to hesitate
before acting

If I were you, I'd think twice about giving up your job – you might not get another one.

17 **to think better of** (sth)
to realise that something you were
intending to do is a bad idea

I was going to say something rude to him, but I thought better of it because I didn't want an argument.

18 **to rule** (s.o./sth) **out**
to decide that someone or
something cannot be considered as
a possibility

I had to rule out living in that country because I couldn't get a visa./The police have ruled him out of their investigation.

19 **to be out**
to be considered to be impossible
or unacceptable

What shall we do tonight? The cinema's out because I've already been three times this week. How about a concert?

20 **not to bargain for** (sth)
not to take something into account
(often something unpleasant)

I was late because I didn't bargain for the train breaking down.

Unit 39 Exercises

39.1 *For each of the sentences below, write a new sentence as similar as possible in meaning to the original sentence, but using the word given. This word must not be altered in any way.*

EXAMPLE   It's no use arguing: I've made up my mind.
point

ANSWER   *There's no point in arguing; I've made up my mind.*

1   You should think about the price before you decide whether to buy it or not.
consideration

....

2   He's not sure whether to go or not.
minds

....

3   I've considered the advantages and disadvantages and I've decided not to go.
weighed

....

4   Considering that she's only just started, she's doing very well.
bearing

....

5   She's not sure whether she wants to marry him or not now.
second

....

6   They will consider age and experience when they decide the salary.
account

....

7   I was going to argue with him, but I decided that it was a bad idea.
better

....

8   I'm not considering that suggestion.
out

....

9   I'm thinking that I might leave the country, but I haven't decided yet.
considering

....

10   When I agreed to do this, I didn't think that it would be so expensive.
bargain

....

11   I'm planning to sell this car and buy another one.
thinking

....

39.2 *Fill each of the blanks with one suitable word.*

1 All things .... , I've quite enjoyed myself here.

2 You should .... twice about lending him all that money.

3 It looks like suicide, although the police have not ruled .... murder.

4 When you said you wanted me to lend you some money, how much did you have in .... ?

5 You don't have to decide immediately. Think it .... for a few days and let me know by Friday.

6 The flight gets in at nine o'clock, so allowing .... passports and customs, I should be out of the airport by ten o'clock.

7 On .... thoughts, I will have another drink.

8 Please be patient and make .... for the fact that she's not well.

9 I've .... my mind – I don't want to go now.

Unit 40 Intelligent/Sensible

1 **intelligent**
having or showing the mental ability to analyse and understand etc.

He hasn't got many qualifications but he's intelligent./She made some intelligent comments at the meeting.

2 **intelligence**
the mental ability to analyse and understand

Someone with her intelligence is bound to get a good job.

3 **clever**
a intelligent; able to learn and understand quickly

She was always very clever at school.

b showing mental or practical ability

She's very clever with her hands.

4 **bright**
clever; mentally quick

She's one of the brightest students in the class.

5 **smart**
(*sometimes derogatory*) clever, especially in knowing how to deal with situations

Doing that course was a smart idea, as it helped him to get a better job./You think you're really smart, don't you? Well, you're not.

6 **brilliant**
extremely clever

He was a brilliant student, the best in the school.

7 **a genius**
an exceptionally brilliant person

Mozart was a child genius.

8 **perceptive**
able to notice and understand things quickly, especially things which other people might not notice

She was perceptive enough to realise right from the start that he was lying.

9 **sharp**
mentally quick or perceptive (often in reacting to situations)

He's so sharp that you can't fool him./She's got a sharp mind.

10 **educated**
having had a good education

Although he's well-educated, he doesn't have a very good job.

11 **sensible**
having or showing common sense

She's sensible enough to be left alone to look after the rest of the children./It's sensible to wear warm clothes when the weather's cold.

12 **common sense**
natural and practical intelligence

You don't have to be clever to do this, it's simply a matter of common sense./Don't keep asking me how to do it – use your common sense!

13 **practical**

    a (of a person) sensible; able to deal with the realities of life

    Be practical – we can't possibly afford to buy a new car./ I'm not at all practical – I can't even change a plug.

    b (of an idea etc.) able to be done in real circumstances

    It wouldn't be practical to live there – it's much too far to travel to work.

14 **realistic**

    practical and sensible (because you understand and accept the facts about a situation)

    It isn't realistic to expect to learn everything in a short time.

15 **down-to-earth**

    paying attention to practical matters and the realities of life, rather than abstract ideas

    He's down-to-earth enough to realise that he won't succeed without hard work.

16 **to have your feet on the ground**

    to have a realistic and sensible attitude to life

    She never spends more money than she can afford because she's got her feet on the ground.

17 **wise**

    using intelligence and experience to make sensible judgements

    Because he's wise I always ask my father for advice./I think it's wise to wait for a while before making a decision.

18 **shrewd**

    having or showing good judgement and ability to analyse situations well, especially in matters which can be turned to your own advantage

    He's a shrewd businessman./He has made some very shrewd deals.

Unit 40 Exercises

40.1 *Choose the word or phrase (A, B, C or D) which best completes each sentence.*

1 I think you'd be .... to leave now. It looks like there's going to be trouble.
    A realistic B wise C shrewd D intelligent

2 She has made some very .... investments, which have earned her a lot of money.
    A bright B practical C shrewd D genial

3 He's very .... and has never had any trouble passing exams.
    A sensible B perceptive C clever D sharp

4 She's quite .... and is certainly capable of doing a more demanding job than the one she's doing now.
    A wise B bright C practical D sensible

5 It was very .... of you to notice the mistake – I don't think anyone else did.
    A sharp B sensible C intelligent D wise

6 He's a .... scientist, one of the best in his field.
   A genius   B practical   C smart   D brilliant

7 She won't be influenced by his ridiculous ideas. She's got her feet ....
   A on earth   B down to earth   C on the ground   D in the ground

8 If you're so .... , then why did you fail your English exam?
   A practical   B shrewd   C perceptive   D smart

9 I think she's .... – her books are brilliant.
   A genial   B a genie   C a genus   D a genius

10 For someone who is in such a responsible position, he is surprisingly lacking in ....
   A sensibility   B common sense   C sensation   D sentiment

11 She's a very .... person, so her friends often go to her for advice.
   A down-to-earth   B basic   C earthy   D practised

40.2 *The word in capitals at the end of each of the following sentences can be used to form a word that fits suitably in the blank space. Fill each blank in this way.*

   EXAMPLE We had an interesting *discussion* about football.   DISCUSS

1 Don't you think it would be .... to see a doctor?   SENSE

2 Don't try to do things too quickly. Set yourself .... targets.   REAL

3 He is of above average ....   INTELLIGENT

4 She is a highly- .... woman.   EDUCATION

5 Be .... – we can't afford to have children just yet.   PRACTICE

6 She's got a very .... mind.   PERCEIVE

Unit 41 Stupid/Naive

1 **stupid**
unintelligent

He's too stupid to understand what's really happening./ Don't be stupid! You're talking rubbish./It was stupid of me to say that because it upset her./It was a stupid thing to say.

2 **thick**
(*colloquial*) (of a person) stupid

I think she's a bit thick – it takes her ages to understand even the most simple things.

3 **slow**
unintelligent; unable to understand things quickly

He's rather slow, so you have to repeat things to him several times before he understands them.

4 **to be slow on the uptake**
slow to understand something obvious

You're a bit slow on the uptake, aren't you? Can't you see he's joking?

5 **foolish**
showing stupidity; doing something without thinking about the consequences

It was foolish of you to spend so much money.

6 **a fool**
a stupid person; someone lacking in intelligence or common sense

He must be a fool to ignore such a fantastic opportunity.

7 **idiotic**
very stupid

It's idiotic to spend so much money on something so useless.

8 **an idiot**
a very stupid person

Only an idiot could make such a stupid mistake./He's an idiot to turn down such a good offer.

9 **silly**
not sensible; rather stupid

That's a silly idea – it won't work./It was silly of me to drink so much – I feel awful now.

10 **daft**
(*colloquial*) silly; foolish

I've forgotten my keys. How daft of me!

11 **ridiculous**
very silly, unreasonable and illogical

It's ridiculous that you have to fill in so many forms for such a simple thing.

12 **ludicrous**
extremely ridiculous

What a ludicrous idea!

13 **absurd**
extremely ridiculous

Don't be absurd! It's much too far to walk.

14 **naive**
innocent, lacking experience and tending to be foolish

He's so naive that everyone takes advantage of him./I realise now that I was naive to trust him.

15 **gullible**
believing everything that you are
told

You must be very gullible if you believe what those politicians are telling you.

16 **impressionable**
easily influenced by other people

He's very impressionable and tends to copy the older boys at school.

17 **impractical**
not sensible, realistic or practical
(of actions or ideas)

It would be impractical to take the car, because there's nowhere to park it.

18 **unrealistic**
not realistic; not considering the
practical facts of a situation

It's unrealistic to expect everyone to be honest.

19 **unwise**
not sensible (of actions or ideas);
foolish and likely to have a bad
result

It would be unwise to make a decision too quickly.

20 **to have your head in the clouds**
to be unaware of the realities of
life

He doesn't realise his plan is impossible because he's got his head in the clouds.

21 **to live in a fantasy world**
to be unaware of the realities of
life; to have very unrealistic ideas

He's living in a fantasy world – he thinks he's going to be rich in three weeks.

Unit 41 Exercises

41.1 *Choose the word or phrase (A, B, C or D) which best completes each sentence.*

1 I don't know why I made such a(n) .... mistake.
A unwise   B thick   C stupid   D gullible

2 'Do storks really bring the babies?' she asked in her typically .... fashion.
A impractical   B absurd   C naive   D impressionable

3 He's not very intelligent, in fact you could call him ....
A silly   B unwise   C daft   D thick

4 You'd have to be very .... to believe everything you read in the papers.
A ridiculous   B gullible   C absurd   D slow

5 I was a bit .... – it took me ages to get the joke.
A silly   B daft   C slow   D unrealistic

6 The decision to invest her money in such a disreputable company was extremely ....
A unwise   B thick   C gullible   D impractical

7 'What .... put salt in my coffee?' he exclaimed.
A fool   B foolish   C stupid   D stupidity

8 It was a(n) .... conversation. We were both talking about different things without realising it.
   A thick   B absurd   C unwise   D foolish

9 You must have your head in the .... if you think you're going to succeed without hard work.
   A clouds   B ground   C sky   D air

10 How .... of me! I've locked myself out of my flat!
   A thick   B unwise   C silly   D naive

11 Don't be .... ! Of course we can't afford such an expensive hotel.
   A daft   B slow   C naive   D gullible

12 You look .... in those shorts! They're much too big for you.
   A impractical   B unwise   C unrealistic   D ludicrous

13 He's at a very .... age and just tends to follow all the other boys.
   A impressive   B impressionist   C impressionable   D impressing

14 If he thinks he's capable of building a house on his own, he's living ....
   A in the clouds   B in a fantasy world   C on the moon   D in the sky

15 I was too slow on the .... to realise that he was trying to trick me.
   A intake   B uptake   C take over   D out-take

41.2 *The word in capitals at the end of each of the following sentences can be used to form a word that fits suitably in the blank space. Fill each blank in this way.*

   EXAMPLE We had an interesting *discussion* about football.   DISCUSS

1 It would be .... to make a decision too quickly.   FOOL

2 What an .... thing to do!   IDIOT

3 It's a good idea in theory, but rather ....   PRACTICE

4 That's the most .... thing I've ever heard.   RIDICULE

5 It would be .... to expect to go straight from
leaving school into a managerial position.   REAL

Unit 42 Remember/Remind/Forget

1 **to remember**
    a (s.o./sth/*doing* sth/*that* ...)
    to bring back to mind (people or events from the past, information etc.); to be still able to think about or visualise someone or something from the past

Of course I remember you, it's Shaun, isn't it?/He suddenly remembered that it was his wife's birthday, and he hadn't even bought her a card./Can you remember what she said?/I don't remember seeing him before./I distinctly remember you saying that I could have the car today.

    b (sth/*to do* sth)
    to be careful not to forget

'Did you remember the eggs?' – 'Oh no, I knew there was something else I was supposed to buy.'/You will remember to feed the cat while I'm on holiday, won't you?

2 **a memory**
    a (*for* sth)
    the ability to remember

You'll have to excuse her. She's got a very bad memory for names./Although he's over eighty, he's still got a very good memory.

    b (*of* sth)
    (usually used in the plural) something that you remember

I've got fond memories of my time there./This place brings back happy memories.

3 **to recall** (sth/*doing* sth)
    to remember (information, past actions, events etc.), by thinking hard

I'm sorry but I don't recall your name./I don't recall saying that./He can't recall when it happened.

4 **to have no recollection** (*of* sth/*of doing* sth)
    to be unable to remember (past actions, events etc.)

I have no recollection of being here before.

5 **to look back** (*on* sth)
    to think about things from your past

She looked back on her childhood with a mixture of happiness and regret.

6 **to remind** (s.o. *of/about* sth; s.o. *to do* sth)
    to make someone remember something (especially by saying something to them)

I'm afraid I've forgotten your name – would you remind me of it?/Could you remind Roger about the party on Friday?/Will you remind me to phone Jenny later?

7 **to remind** (s.o.) **of** (s.o./sth)
    to cause someone to think about something (often by appearing to be similar)

The painting reminds me of another one in the National Gallery./Doesn't Rosemary remind you of her mother?/This record always reminds me of our holiday in France.

8 **to recognise** (s.o./sth)
    to know that someone or something is the same as someone or something previously seen, heard or experienced

I recognise her from photographs I've seen./She didn't recognise his voice over the phone.

9 **to ring a bell**
to remind you of something; to be or sound familiar

I'm not sure if I know him or not but his name rings a bell./Her face rings a bell, but I can't remember from where.

10 **to jog someone's memory**
to help someone to remember something

The police hoped that taking him back to the scene of the crime might help to jog his memory about what happened that night.

11 **to make a note** (*of* sth)
to write something down so that you will remember it

I made a note of his number in case I ever needed to phone him.

12 **to know/learn** (sth) **by heart**
to know or learn something very well so that you can repeat it perfectly from memory

I learnt the words to the song by heart./He knows the poem by heart.

13 **to forget**
a (sth/*to do* sth/*that* ...)
to fail to remember something

I'm afraid I've forgotten your name./Don't forget to turn the lights out./She completely forgot that she had arranged to meet him./'Did you video that programme for me?' – 'Oh, sorry, I forgot.'

b (*about* s.o./sth)
to put someone or something out of your mind and stop thinking about them

If you still think we're going to America for our holidays, then forget (about) it./If I were you, I'd forget (about) him.

14 **forgetful**
having the tendency to forget

He's become very forgetful in his old age.

15 **absent-minded**
forgetful, often because you are too busy thinking about other things

My grandfather is terribly absent-minded; he's always forgetting where he's put things.

16 **to leave** (sth *behind*/sth somewhere)
to forget to bring or take something with you

We'll have to go back – I've left my wallet behind./Somebody's left their umbrella behind./I'm always leaving my keys (behind) at the office.

17 **to be unable to place** (s.o.)
to be unable to remember where or when you last saw or heard someone

I know her face but I can't place her./I'm sure I recognise that voice, but I can't quite place it.

18 **to be on the tip of your tongue**
to be something (a word, name etc.) that you can almost but not quite remember

What's his name? It's on the tip of my tongue.

19 **to slip your mind**
   to be forgotten (temporarily) by
   you (especially something that
   you were supposed to do)

Sorry I wasn't at the meeting last night. It completely slipped my mind./I'm sorry I didn't phone you – it slipped my mind.

20 **to go**
   to disappear from your memory

I've been trying to remember the title of that book but it's gone.

21 **to go blank**
   to completely forget what was in
   your mind; to be unable to think

I knew the subject really well, but as soon as I got in the examination hall, my mind went blank./I was so nervous during the interview that I went completely blank – I couldn't even remember the name of my previous employer.

Unit 42 Exercises

42.1 *Choose the word or phrase (A, B, C or D) which best completes each sentence.*

1 She has no .... of saying such a thing.
   A recollection   B reminder   C souvenir   D memory

2 I've got a good .... for faces.
   A recollection   B remembrance   C souvenir   D memory

3 My .... of childhood are happy ones.
   A memoirs   B reminders   C souvenirs   D memories

4 I hope you didn't forget .... the plants while I was away.
   A to water   B watering   C water   D having watered

5 The actress wore dark glasses to avoid being ....
   A recalled   B remembered   C reminded   D recognised

6 Could you .... him to bring his camera?
   A recall   B remember   C remind   D recognise

7 Did you .... to lock the door?
   A recall   B remember   C remind   D recognise

8 Who does Barbara .... you of?
   A recall   B remember   C remind   D recognise

9 What was his name again? It's .... completely.
   A slipped   B gone   C flown   D left

42.2 *Fill each of the blanks with one suitable word.*

1 I intended to pay my phone bill, but it .... my mind because I was so busy.

2 I can't find my keys. I must have .... them in the car.

3 She's the most .... person I know. One of these days she'll forget her head!

4 I don't .... agreeing to do that. Are you sure I did?

5 When I look .... those terrible times, I can't believe I survived!

6 I know all of the words to this song .... I can sing it to you now if you like.

7 He's so absent- .... that he went to work the other day in his slippers!

42.3 *For each of the sentences below, write a new sentence as similar as possible in meaning to the original sentence, but using the word given. This word must not be altered in any way.*

EXAMPLE It's no use arguing: I've made up my mind.
point

ANSWER *There's no point in arguing; I've made up my mind.*

1 I'll write your address down in case I need to write to you.
note

....

2 Let me give you a clue to help you remember.
jog

....

3 I've completely forgotten what I was going to say.
blank

....

4 I can very nearly remember the word.
tongue

....

5 I remember this song from somewhere.
bell

....

6 I can't remember when or where I've met him.
place

....

Unit 43 Understand/Realise

Part 1

1 **to get** (sth)
  to understand

I don't get it. Why did he behave in such a peculiar way?/ I explained it very carefully, but he still didn't seem to get what I was saying./She didn't laugh because she didn't get the joke.

2 **to see**
  to understand (what someone means or what they are telling you)

'I'm afraid you'll have to wait until Friday for an appointment.' – 'Oh, I see.'/Can't you see that it's a completely impossible suggestion?/I see what you mean about him. He is rather bad-tempered, isn't he?

3 **to follow** (s.o./sth)
  to understand the development of something (a story, explanation etc.)

I couldn't follow the story – there were too many things happening at once./Do you follow me?

4 **to be with** (s.o.)
  to understand what someone is talking about

Yes, I'm with you. Carry on./I'm afraid I'm not with you. Could you start again?

5 **to get the gist** (*of* sth)
  to understand the general meaning or main points of something said or written

He spoke very quickly, but I got the gist of what he was saying.

6 **to see/get someone's point**
  to understand the main idea of what someone is saying; to understand someone's opinion

I see your point, but I still don't agree with you./Do you get my point?

7 **to get someone's drift**
  to understand the general meaning of what someone is saying

'What I'm trying to say is that we're all treated rather unfairly' – 'Yes, I get your drift.'

8 **to make sense**
  to be logical or understandable

Does that make sense? Do you understand what I'm saying?/Your essay doesn't make much sense./I don't know why he lost his temper. It doesn't make any sense.

9 **to make of** (s.o./sth)
  (usually used after 'what') to understand by or interpret from

What do you make of the latest news? Do you think it's good or bad?/I don't know what to make of his comment. I don't know if he was joking or not./No one really knows what to make of her.

10 **to gather** (*from* s.o./sth; *that* ...)
  to understand because of information received

I gather from Richard that you're looking for another place to live./I gather you phoned me earlier – what did you want?

11 **to get through** (*to* s.o.)
  to make someone understand

I can't seem to get through to him that he's making a terrible mistake.

12 **to misunderstand** (s.o.)
to understand wrongly

Don't misunderstand me. I'm not criticising you, I'm trying to help you.

13 **a misunderstanding**
a failure to understand something correctly

I'm afraid there's been a misunderstanding. Mr Bradshaw wasn't expecting you until tomorrow.

14 **to miss the point**
to fail to understand the main idea of what someone is saying

No, you've missed my point; I wasn't saying that moving house was a bad idea, just that it would be difficult at the moment.

15 **to be unable to make head or tail of** (sth)
to be completely unable to understand something; to be totally confused by something

I can't make head or tail of this form. How do I fill it in?

Part 2

1 **to be aware** (*of* sth/*that* ...)
to realise; to have knowledge of something (a fact or situation etc.)

I'm aware that you don't agree with her. You don't have to keep on telling me./Is it really that late? I wasn't aware of the time./He was suddenly aware of somebody following him.

2 **to be well aware** (*of* sth/*that* ...)
to be very aware of something

I'm well aware that it won't be easy./We're well aware of all the problems involved.

3 **to be conscious** (*of* sth/*that* ...)
to be aware of something

People are becoming more and more conscious of the need to protect the environment.

4 **to appreciate** (sth/*that* ...)
to realise or understand fully (especially the circumstances of a particular situation)

I don't think you appreciate the problem./I appreciate that you're busy, but that's no excuse for forgetting his birthday.

5 **to dawn on** (s.o.)
to become known or clear to someone

A few days later, the truth dawned on me./It suddenly dawned on him who she was.

6 **to occur to** (s.o.)
(of an idea or thought) to come suddenly into someone's mind

It occurs to me that I might have made a mistake./It didn't occur to her to get a taxi.

7 **to strike** (s.o.)
to occur to someone powerfully

It strikes me that this is a complete waste of time./An awful thought struck her – did she have enough money to pay for the meal she had just had?

8 **to cross your mind**
to occur to you briefly or suddenly

It crossed my mind that he might be lying./'You think I'm lazy, don't you?' – 'Not at all. The thought never even crossed my mind.'

9 **to be unaware** (*of* sth/*that* ...) not to realise or be aware of something

She was completely unaware of his presence./I was unaware that you felt so strongly about the subject.

10 **to be oblivious** (*to/of* sth) to be unaware of something

He's oblivious to other people's feelings./She was quite oblivious of all the trouble she had caused.

Unit 43 Exercises

43.1 *Choose the word or phrase (A, B, C or D) which best completes each sentence.*

1 I'm afraid .... you. Could you repeat what you just said?
A I don't get   B I'm not with   C I don't see   D I miss

2 I .... it. I thought he was happy here, so why has he left?
A don't get   B can't follow   C misunderstand   D miss

3 'Do you understand what I'm trying to say?' – 'Yes, I .... what you mean.'
A see   B catch   C take   D follow

4 You've all .... the point. The film itself is not racist – it simply tries to make us question our own often racist attitudes.
A mistaken   B missed   C misunderstood   D lost

5 I often wonder what people abroad make .... Britain.
A from   B by   C for   D of

6 I couldn't .... him because he spoke far too quickly.
A gather   B follow   C see   D catch

43.2 *Fill each of the blanks with one suitable word.*

1 There were a few details I didn't understand, but I got the .... of his explanation.

2 You obviously .... me. I meant I'd be there before seven o'clock, not after seven o'clock.

3 We were conscious .... a change in their attitude towards us.

4 She thinks the book is offensive to women, and I can .... her point.

5 It was just a .... He thought I'd insulted him, but in fact I hadn't.

6 It was impossible to get .... him how stupid he was being.

43.3 *Finish each of the following sentences in such a way that it means exactly the same as the sentence printed before it.*

EXAMPLE   Who owns that car?

ANSWER   *Who does that car belong to?*

1 I don't understand a single word of this letter.
I can't make head..

2 She fully understands that she will have to work hard.
She's well ....

3 He suddenly thought that he might have misunderstood her.
   It crossed ....

4 He never thought of telling her.
   It never occurred ....

5 That sentence doesn't have an understandable meaning.
   That sentence makes ....

6 He didn't know about her feelings for him.
   He was unaware ....

43.4 *For each of the sentences below, write a new sentence as similar as possible in meaning to the original sentence, but using the word given. This word must not be altered in any way.*

   EXAMPLE   It's no use arguing: I've made up my mind.
             point
   ANSWER   *There's no point in arguing; I've made up my mind.*

1 Although I don't speak Italian very well, I understood the general meaning of what she said.
   drift

   ....

2 I'm fully aware of the fact that it's not your fault.
   appreciate

   ....

3 He doesn't realise what other people are saying about him.
   oblivious

   ....

4 From what I read in the paper, the economic situation is getting worse.
   gather

   ....

5 The way I see it, there's only one thing you can do.
   strikes

   ....

6 He didn't realise the cost involved in buying a house.
   aware

   ....

7 After a while, I realised that I'd made a terrible mistake.
   dawned

   ....

Section E
Communicating

Units 44-46

Unit 44 Agree/Co-operate/Disagree/Argue _____

Part 1

1 **to agree**
  a (*with* s.o.; *about*/*on* sth; *that* ...) to (say that you) have the same opinion as someone else

I agree with her on most things./I agree with you about not making a decision too quickly./She agrees that the whole thing is her fault.

  b (*to* sth/*to do* sth) to say yes to something

He wouldn't agree to the terms of the contract./They agreed to give me my money back because it had been their mistake.

  c (*with* sth) to support or approve of (a moral issue etc.)

I don't agree with violence in any circumstances.

2 **to be in agreement**
  (*formal*) to agree

They're in complete agreement on the matter.

3 **agreed**
  I agree (used when you have reached a joint decision with someone about something)

'If you cook, I'll do the washing-up.' – 'Agreed.'

4 **to come to/reach an agreement**
  to agree after discussion

We reached an agreement that we would take it in turns to cook./They came to an agreement not to discuss the subject again.

5 **to be in favour** (*of* sth/*of doing* sth)
  to support something; to think that something is a good idea

The majority of workers were in favour of strike action./ I'm in favour of leaving now./Hands up all those in favour.

6 **to accept**
  a (sth) to say yes (to an offer etc.)

If they make me a good enough offer I'll accept it./He asked her to marry him and she accepted straightaway.

  b (sth/*that* ...) to agree or recognize that something is true

I accept that you were right./She still can't accept that he's dead./He refuses to accept the fact that he's wrong.

7 **to compromise** (*with* s.o.)
  to reach an agreement between two extremes

I'll compromise with you – you can have the car this weekend if I can have it next weekend.

8 **to reach a compromise**
  to compromise after discussion

We couldn't agree at the beginning but eventually we reached a compromise.

9 **to meet** (s.o.) **halfway**
  to compromise with someone

You'll have to meet him halfway – you won't get everything you want.

10 **to co-operate** (*with* s.o.)
to work or act together with
someone; to do what someone
wants in order to help them

He said he was willing to co-operate with them because he didn't want any trouble.

11 **co-operative**
helpful; willing to co-operate

The secretary wasn't very co-operative and wouldn't give me the information I wanted.

12 **co-operation**
the act of co-operating

Thanks to their co-operation, we solved the problem.

Part 2

1 **to disagree**
   a (*with* s.o. *on/about* sth)
   to (say that you) have a different
   opinion from someone else

We're good friends, even though we often disagree./I disagree with him about what the best thing to do is.

   b (*with* sth)
   to believe that something is wrong

I disagree with the Government's education policy.

2 **to have a disagreement** (*with* s.o.
about sth)
(*formal*) to disagree verbally

I had a disagreement with the boss about the work I was doing, so I left.

3 **to contradict** (s.o.)
to disagree by saying the exact
opposite; to tell someone that they
are wrong

I can't say anything without him contradicting me.

4 **to dispute** (sth)
(*formal*) to believe that something
isn't true or right

I dispute the official version of what happened.

5 **to object** (*to* sth/*to doing* sth)
to feel that something is wrong
and not to like it

I object to the way the boss treats me./I don't object to them coming with us.

6 **an objection** (*to* sth/*to doing* sth)
a reason to disagree; a statement
of disagreement

There were many objections to the council's plans./I have no objection to them staying with us.

7 **to be opposed** (*to* sth/*to doing*
sth)
to disagree strongly with or be
against something, often for moral
reasons

The Catholic Church is opposed to divorce./His parents are opposed to him giving up his education.

8 **opposition** (*to* sth)
strong disagreement

There is a lot of opposition to the government's defence policy.

9 **to argue** (*with* s.o./*about* sth)
to disagree verbally with
someone, often angrily

Don't argue with me!/They're always arguing about money.

10 **to have an argument** (*with* s.o./
about sth)
to argue

I had an argument with him yesterday about the best way to do the job.

11 **to row** (*with* s.o./*about* sth)
to argue noisily and sometimes
violently (often involving people
who know each other well)

She often rows with him in public.

12 **to have a row** (*with* s.o./*about*
sth)
to row

I had a row with her and now she refuses to speak to me./ They have a lot of rows about money.

13 **to quarrel** (*with* s.o./*about* sth)
to argue angrily, often about small
things

The children often quarrel about which programme they're going to watch on TV.

14 **to have a quarrel**
to quarrel

They've had a quarrel so they're not very friendly with each other now.

15 **to bicker** (*about* sth)
to argue like children, about small
things

Will you two stop bickering and let me get some sleep!/ They're always bickering about whose turn it is to do the washing up.

16 **controversial**
causing argument

It was a controversial film which shocked many people.

Unit 44 Exercises

44.1 *Choose the word or phrase (A, B, C or D) which best completes each sentence.*

1 They're like children. They .... about the most stupid little things.
   A dispute   B contradict   C oppose   D bicker

2 They were .... about who should make the coffee.
   A quarrelling   B disputing   C objecting   D opposing

3 I'm not .... them staying with us, as long as it's only for a few days.
   A disagreed with   B opposite   C opposed to   D objected to

4 They had a(n) .... and never spoke to each other again.
   A dispute   B objection   C quarrel   D opposition

5 'So, we're going to Italy for our holidays, right?' – '.............. . Now whereabouts in Italy shall we go?'
   A Agree   B I'm agree   C Agreed   D In agreement

6 The players .... the referee's decision.
   A disagreed   B disputed   C objected   D contradicted

44.2 *Fill each of the blanks with one suitable word.*

1 You've just .... yourself. You said the opposite a few minutes ago.

2 We discussed it for a while and then we .... an agreement.

3 I think you should try to .... with him. You can't both have everything you want.

4 I don't .... that. I don't think it's true at all.

5 He wasn't at all .... He wouldn't do anything I asked him to do.

6 Thank you for your invitation which we are pleased to ....

7 We look forward to many more years of .... between our two countries.

8 It is a .... new law, which many people disagree with.

9 She argues .... me .... almost everything.

10 I agree .... you .... what the problem is.

11 I've never had the slightest disagreement .... him .... anything.

12 I hate to say it, but I disagree .... you completely.

44.3 *For each of the sentences below, write a new sentence as similar as possible in meaning to the original sentence, but using the word given. This word must not be altered in any way.*

EXAMPLE   It's no use arguing: I've made up my mind.
    point

ANSWER   *There's no point in arguing; I've made up my mind.*
....

1 I don't mind changing my plans.
objection

....

2 I thought about it for a while and then I accepted their offer.
agreed

....

3 The neighbours were arguing.
row

....

4 Do we agree?
agreement

....

5 I don't like having to pay so much for so little.
object

....

6 He thinks that divorce is wrong.
agree

....

7 I don't want to argue with you.
argument

....

8 In the end we found a solution that suited us both.
compromise

....

9 I don't think that the way he treats people is right.
disagree

....

10 I'll compromise with you.
meet

....

11 We've agreed to share the cost.
come

....

12 I expressed my disagreement with his plan.
opposition

....

13 He thinks that capital punishment is a good idea.
favour

....

14 If you do what I ask, everything will be all right.
co-operate

....

15 I never have arguments with my parents.
row

....

Unit 45 Show/Prove

1 **to show**
   a (s.o. sth/*that* ...)
   to allow or cause something to be seen

   They showed me their holiday photographs./Her face showed that she was upset.

   b to be visible or able to be seen

   She wore a hat and a scarf, so that only her eyes were showing./She didn't let her anger show./I've tried to clean the dirt off my jacket. Does it still show?

2 **to indicate**
   a (sth/*that* ...)
   to suggest or show the possibility or probability of something

   The clouds seemed to indicate rain./Her tone of voice indicated that she was angry.

   b (sth)
   to show by pointing

   'Sit down' he said, indicating the chair in the corner.

3 **to reveal** (sth/*that* ...)
   to allow something previously secret, unknown or out of sight to be known or seen

   He revealed that he had never really liked her./A nationwide survey has revealed that three out of every four people are dissatisfied with their jobs./She took off her hat to reveal a mass of curls.

4 **to disclose** (sth)
   to reveal private information

   He refused to disclose his income.

5 **to give** (sth) **away**
   to reveal the truth about something (especially something that you are trying to hide)

   The expression on his face gave away his real feelings.

6 **to expose** (s.o./sth)
   to reveal the truth about someone or something (especially when it involves a crime or scandal)

   On tonight's programme we expose the truth about the Minister and the former model.

7 **to let on**
   to reveal a secret

   He must have known the truth but he didn't let on./If I tell you, do you promise not to let on?

8 **to come out**
   to be revealed

   Eventually it came out that he'd been lying all the time.

9 **to convey** (sth)
   to make known or to communicate (ideas, thoughts, feelings etc.)

   The film conveys the horror of war like no other film I've seen./He conveyed his anger by glaring at me.

10 **to point** (sth) **out** (*to* s.o.)
   to show or tell someone something that they hadn't previously noticed or known

   He pointed out some interesting buildings during the journey./I should point out to you that this is only a suggestion, so please feel free to criticise./As I pointed out last week, there are just too many problems involved.

11 **to prove** (sth/*that* ...)
to show that something is true or correct

Your results prove that you haven't been working hard enough./The witness's statement proved his innocence.

12 **proof** (*of* sth/*that* ...)
something that shows that something is true; documents, information etc. that prove something

Keep the receipt as proof that you paid the bill./The police suspect him but they have no proof./I had to show them my passport as proof of identity.

13 **it (just) goes to show**
it proves

He's rich but unhappy. It (just) goes to show that money isn't everything.

14 **a sign** (*of* sth/*that* ...)
something that shows you or gives you an idea of the presence of something else

When he starts shouting, it's a sign that he's drunk./Expensive jewellery is a sign of wealth.

15 **an indication** (*of* sth/*that* ...)
something that indicates something else; a sign or suggestion

The expression on his face was an indication of his mood./All the indications are that the union will accept the offer of a ten per cent pay increase.

16 **indicative of** (sth)
(*formal*) showing or suggesting

His nasty comments about her are indicative of his attitude towards women in general.

17 **a gesture**
a a movement of the body, especially the hands, to indicate an idea or feeling

He raised his fist in a gesture of defiance./He made a rude gesture with his fingers to show that he didn't like me.

b something that is done as an indication of (often friendly) intentions

I bought them a present as a gesture of thanks.

18 **to nod/shake your head**
to indicate 'yes' or 'no' by moving your head

She nodded her head in agreement./When he asked her if she wanted to go, she shook her head firmly.

19 **to shrug your shoulders**
to raise your shoulders to show that you are not interested in something, do not care or do not know

When I asked him for his opinion he just shrugged his shoulders.

20 **to pull a face**
to make a twisted, ugly expression on your face in order to show your dislike or disgust, or possibly to cause laughter

When she told him to do the washing-up, he pulled a face./She pulled a face to make the little boy laugh.

21 **to hide** (sth *from* s.o.)

    a to put something where it cannot be seen or found

        I hid her present in the wardrobe./She wants me to give up smoking, so she has hidden my cigarettes.

    b to keep something (information, feelings etc.) secret

        She was unable to hide her disappointment./He accused her of hiding the facts from him.

Unit 45 Exercises

45.1 *Choose the word or phrase (A, B, C or D) which best completes each sentence.*

1 She .... the money so that no one would be able to find it.
  A let on   B disclosed   C conveyed   D hid

2 He .... that he hadn't left the job; he'd been sacked.
  A revealed   B conveyed   C showed   D exposed

3 It's difficult to .... the atmosphere of Paris to somone who hasn't been there.
  A point out   B disclose   C convey   D indicate

4 The report .... the corruption in the Government.
  A conveyed   B exposed   C let on   D indicated

5 I asked him, but he wouldn't .... how much he'd paid for it.
  A convey   B disclose   C come out   D show

6 I know you weren't enjoying yourself, but you shouldn't have .... it; that was rude.
  A given away   B shown   C exposed   D disclosed

7 He paid me some money in advance as .... that he was honest.
  A gesture   B indication   C test   D proof

8 The expression on his face .... that he was rather worried.
  A gestured   B indicated   C came out   D pointed out

9 I know he stole the money, but I can't .... it because I didn't actually see him.
  A indicate   B expose   C prove   D reveal

10 When questioned about the Government's defence plans, the Minister gave very little ....
  A out   B up   C away   D off

11 He showed no .... of nervousness.
  A sign   B signal   C gesture   D proof

12 I invited them to dinner as a .... of friendship.
  A gesture   B signal   C sample   D proof

13 She kept smiling because she didn't want to .... that she found him boring.
  A give away   B point out   C let on   D come out

45.2 *Fill each of the blanks with one suitable word.*

1 It has recently come .... that the Government's version of events was untrue.

2 She obviously didn't care because she simply .... her shoulders.

3 Don't just sit there and .... your head. If you don't agree, tell me why.

4 If you hadn't pointed .... where I was going wrong, I'd never have known.

5 Her kindness towards you is indicative .... her caring nature.

6 Since he .... his head, I assumed that he agreed.

7 I thought he was honest. It just goes .... that people are seldom what they seem.

8 He .... a face when his mother told him to tidy his room because he didn't want to do it.

9 He made a .... with his hand to show that he wanted me to follow him.

10 I felt that the people I talked to on my first day there gave me an .... what the company was really like.

Unit 46 Suggest

1 **a suggestion**
something that is suggested; an
idea or plan

What are we going to do tonight? Does anyone have any suggestions?

2 **to make a suggestion**

Can I make a suggestion? Why don't you try to do it this way?

3 **to imply** (sth/*that* ...)
to suggest indirectly

His silence on the matter seemed to imply agreement./I got annoyed because he seemed to be implying that I wasn't telling the truth.

4 **an implication**
something that is implied

They didn't give me a definite answer, but the implication was that I would get the job.

5 **not in as/so many words**
not directly, but suggested

She didn't say it in as many words, but I got the impression that she was very unhappy.

6 **to hint** (*at* sth/*that* ...)
to suggest or mention indirectly
that something is the case, or that
you want something

He hinted that I should leave by looking at his watch./The Prime Minister hinted that there would have to be changes./She hinted at the possibility of change.

7 **to drop a hint**
to suggest something indirectly
(hoping that it will be understood)

Helen has dropped a hint that she wants me to buy her a watch for Christmas.

8 **a clue**
something that suggests the
answer to a question or problem

The police searched the area but couldn't find any clues.

9 **to give** (s.o.) **a clue**
to tell someone something to help
them find the answer to a question
or problem

I don't know the answer. Give me a clue – what's the first letter?

10 **to guess** (sth)
to suggest an answer without
knowing if it is correct

He guessed my height correctly./'Guess how old she is?' – 'I don't know. About thirty five?'

11 **a guess**
a suggested answer or idea, of
which you are not sure

This is just a guess but I think it might cost you about £100./If you're not sure of an answer, it's always better to have a guess than to write nothing.

12 **to propose**
a (sth/*that* ...)
(*formal*) to suggest (a plan or
idea) for consideration

I propose that we have a meeting tomorrow to discuss this matter further./The Soviet Union has proposed further talks on arms reductions.

b (*to* s.o.)
to suggest marriage

He proposed to her in the restaurant, and she agreed immediately.

13 **advice**
suggestion(s) about what someone should do (often given by someone who knows more)

He asked a lawyer for advice./I don't know what to do – I need some advice./She took the doctor's advice and stayed in bed.

14 **a tip**
a small but useful suggestion or piece of advice (often from an expert)

The book contains lots of good tips for anyone thinking of starting their own business./Let me give you a tip. If you want to improve your English, read an English newspaper.

15 **to warn** (s.o. *to do* sth/ s.o. *that* ...)
to suggest strongly that something is dangerous or that something bad may happen (especially if someone does or does not do something)

The policeman warned them that the roads were wet./My parents warned me not to talk to strangers when I was a child./She warned him to be careful.

Unit 46 Exercises

46.1 *Choose the word or phrase (A, B, C or D) which best completes each sentence.*

1 If peeling onions makes you cry, a useful .... is to peel them under water.
   A tap   B trap   C tip   D trip

2 The management has .... a new deal which they hope will end the strike.
   A hinted   B proposed   C implied   D warned

3 What exactly are you .... at?
   A hinting   B implying   C suggesting   D proposing

4 The look he gave us seemed to .... disapproval.
   A hint   B imply   C propose   D warn

5 She kept looking at her watch and .... hints that she wanted us to leave.
   A giving   B taking   C doing   D dropping

6 I've no idea how old she is. Give me a .... – is she older or younger than you are?
   A clue   B guess   C tip   D track

46.2 *Fill each of the blanks with one suitable word.*

1 'Did he actually say that?' – 'Well, not .... words, but that was the impression I got.'

2 I .... you not to trust him but you didn't listen to me.

3 He .... her several times before she finally agreed to marry him.

4 He didn't say so directly, but the .... was that I'd be sacked if I was late again.

5 I have a .... Why don't we all go in my car?

6 .... who I saw today? You'll never believe it!

7 She gave me some excellent .... which was very helpful to me.

8 Could I .... a suggestion?

Section F
Doing and Causing

Units 47-50

Unit 47 Encourage/Discourage/Persuade/Force _____

Part 1

1 **to encourage** (s.o. *to do* sth)
to tell someone that what they are doing or want to do is good; to give someone confidence

I did well at school because the teachers encouraged me to work hard.

2 **encouragement**
the act of encouraging

My parents' encouragement gave me the confidence to carry on.

3 **an encouragement**
something which encourages someone

Her words were an encouragement to him.

4 **to support**
  a (s.o.)
  to help or defend someone in a practical way, often verbally

If they criticise you, I'll support you./Her parents support her in every decision she makes.

  b (s.o.)
  to provide money for someone to live on

When I didn't have a job my parents supported me.

  c (sth)
  to agree with or approve of (an idea or proposal etc.)

I don't support the Government's education policy.

  d (s.o./sth)
  to follow or be loyal to (a sports team etc.)

Which football team do you support?

5 **to back** (s.o.) **up**
to support someone who is in a difficult situation

If there's an argument, I'll back you up.

6 **to give** (s.o.) **moral support**
to support someone by encouraging them, but without giving any practical help

I went with her to the interview to give her moral support.

7 **to discourage** (s.o. *from doing* sth)
to tell someone or cause them to think that what they want to do is a bad idea; to make someone less enthusiastic about something

He discouraged her from giving up her job./Don't be discouraged by the price, it really is worth it.

8 **an incentive** (*to do* sth)
something that encourages you to do something

The prospect of higher wages is an incentive to work harder.

9 **to deter** (s.o. *from doing* sth)
to (try to) stop someone from
doing something, by the threat of
something unpleasant

They have dogs to deter people from breaking in.

10 **a deterrent**
something that deters you from
doing something

Whether capital punishment is really a deterrent, as some people claim, is questionable.

11 **to put** (s.o.) **off** (sth/*doing* sth)
to cause someone not to want to
do something

Your terrible stories about New York have put me off going there.

Part 2

1 **to persuade**
 a (s.o. *to do* sth)
to cause someone to agree to do
something (often by giving
reasons etc.)

At first I didn't agree, but she persuaded me to change my mind./Can't you persuade her to come to the cinema tonight?

 b (s.o. *that* ...)
to make someone believe
something (often involving a
discussion)

Eventually she persuaded me that she was right and I was wrong.

2 **to convince**
 a (s.o. *to do* sth)
to persuade someone to do
something

He convinced her to marry him.

 b (s.o. *of* sth/s.o. *that* ...)
to make someone believe that
something is true

She convinced him that she had been telling the truth./She convinced everybody of his guilt.

3 **to urge** (s.o. *to do* sth)
to advise or encourage someone
very strongly to do something

They urged me to get a good education.

4 **to talk** (s.o.) **into** (sth/*doing* sth)
to persuade someone to do
something

She didn't want to go at first but he talked her into it.

5 **to talk** (s.o.) **out of** (sth/*doing* sth)
to persuade someone not to do
something

They talked him out of leaving.

6 **to force** (s.o. *to do* sth)
to make someone do something
that they do not want to do by
ordering them, or making it
impossible for them not to do it

*The thieves forced him to give them his money./I was so
angry that I was forced to say something.*

7 **to push**
  a (s.o. *to do* sth)
to try to force someone to do
something (which they do not
want to do)

They're pushing me to make a decision quickly.

  b (s.o. *into* sth/s.o. *into doing* sth)
to succeed in forcing someone to
do something

*I wanted to turn down the offer, but my family pushed me
into accepting it./I really didn't want to come out tonight,
but Carol pushed me into it.*

8 **to put pressure** (*on* s.o. *to do* sth)
to try to force someone to do
something

*My landlord is putting pressure on me to pay the rent as
I'm three months late.*

9 **to go on** (*at* s.o.)
to talk continually in order to put
pressure on someone to do
something

Stop going on at me! I'll fix the roof when I've got time.

10 **to chase** (s.o.) **up**
to urge or remind someone to do
something that you want them to
do, and that they haven't yet done

*Since they haven't replied to your enquiry I think you'd
better chase them up.*

11 **to impose** (sth *on* s.o.)
to force someone to accept
something (an opinion, belief etc.)

*He always imposes his choice on other people – he never
lets them decide for themselves./They're trying to impose a
no-smoking rule at work.*

12 **to have no choice** (*but to do* sth)
to be forced to do something
because there is no alternative

*The Prime Minister had no choice but to resign./I'm afraid
you have no choice but to accept our recommendations.*

Unit 47 Exercises

47.1 *Finish each of the following sentences in such a way that it means exactly the same as the sentence
printed before it.*

EXAMPLE Who owns that car?
ANSWER *Who does that car belong to?*

1 I was going to leave, but because of what she said, I didn't.
She persuaded ....

2 I didn't want to buy it, but because he insisted, I bought it.
He pushed ....

3 'You must think about it carefully before you decide,' she told me.
She urged ....

4 'I am innocent,' she said, and the court believed her.
She convinced ....

5 She says that it's good if I make my own decisions.
She encourages ....

6 His wife keeps telling him that he should get a better job.
His wife is pushing ....

7 'You're making a terrible mistake,' she told me, and eventually I believed her.
She persuaded ....

8 Why did he decide to go to Italy instead of France?
What convinced ....

47.2 *Fill each of the blanks with one suitable word.*

1 My mother is always going .... at me to give up smoking.

2 The salesman tried to talk her .... buying a set of encyclopaedias.

3 My landlady is chasing me .... about the rent, as it's now three weeks late.

4 His recent car crash has put him .... driving.

5 Happily, the policewoman talked the robber .... shooting his hostage.

47.3 *For each of the sentences below, write a new sentence as similar as possible in meaning to the*
original sentence, but using the word given. This word must not be altered in any way.

EXAMPLE It's no use arguing: I've made up my mind.
point

ANSWER *There's no point in arguing; I've made up my mind.*

1 They have security guards so that people won't try to steal.
discourage

....

2 They're telling me that I must make a decision soon.
pressure

....

3 When I make my complaint, I hope that you'll say you agree with me.
back

....

4 She's always trying to force other people to accept her opinions.
impose

....

205

5 He has always done things to help her in her career.
   supported

   ....

6 He offered them more money to encourage them to do the job quickly.
   incentive

   ....

7 The judge gave a harsh sentence so that other people wouldn't commit the same crime.
   deter

   ....

8 Because of the circumstances, I have to act quickly.
   forced

   ....

9 She was nervous about going to the doctor's, so I went with her so that she wouldn't be alone.
   moral

   ....

10 He doesn't earn enough money to survive.
    support

    ....

11 I need as many people to encourage me as I can get.
    encouragement

    ....

12 Many people believe that the death penalty deters criminals.
    deterrent

    ....

13 I was forced to apologise.
    choice

    ....

14 My favourite cricket team is Hampshire County Cricket Club.
    support

    ....

Unit 48 Influence/Ignore

Part 1

1 **to influence** (s.o./sth)
to cause someone or something to change, behave or happen in a particular way (by using persuasion or suggestion rather than force, or by example)

Children are influenced by their parents./Your advice influenced my decision./His paintings are clearly influenced by the Italian School.

2 **influence** (*on* s.o./sth)
the ability or power to influence someone or something

You only have to look at the way he dresses now, to see how much influence his friends have had on him./He would never have got the job without his father's influence.

3 **an influence** (*on* s.o./sth)
the effect that someone or something has on the way people think or behave, or on what happens; a person or thing that has the power to influence

Her grandmother has a great influence on her./I agree that the portrayal of violence in films can have an influence on our own behaviour./The Rolling Stones have obviously been a big influence on their music.

4 **to affect**
   a (s.o./sth)
   to cause a change in the way people think or act, or in a particular situation

He claims he won't be affected by his new-found wealth./The Government's new law affects a lot of people's lives.

   b (s.o.)
   to cause someone to have feelings of sadness, love, anger etc.

She's so tough that not even the worst things seem to affect her./Although he tries not to show it, I think losing his job has really affected him.

5 **to have an effect** (*on* s.o./sth)
to cause a change; to touch or influence a person's mind, emotions, experience etc.

When his girlfriend left him, it had a terrible effect on his confidence./I tried to persuade her but my words had no effect on her.

6 **to make an impression** (*on* s.o.)
to have a strong effect on someone's mind or feelings

Advertising always tries to make an impression on people.

7 **to make a difference** (*to* s.o./sth)
to influence or change someone or something

Before you decide to get married, don't forget it will make an enormous difference to your lifestyle./The new law makes no difference to me.

8 **to have a bearing** (*on* sth)
to be part of the reason for something; to have some effect on or connection with something

Money wasn't the only reason I took the job but it certainly had a bearing on it.

9 **to play a part** (*in* sth)
to have some effect on something; to be partly responsible for something

Homesickness played a part in his decision to leave.

10 **to have a say** (*in* sth)
to have an influence on something (especially when making a decision)

Money had a say in my choice of career./He has a lot of say in the running of this company.

11 **to contribute** (*to* sth)
to help to cause (an event or situation)

Her acting contributed to the success of the play.

Part 2

1 **to ignore** (s.o./sth)
to behave as if someone or something does not exist (by not reacting); to refuse to be influenced by someone or something

She ignored my advice./I don't know what I've said to upset her, but she completely ignored me this morning./The bank sent me a nasty letter which I ignored.

2 **to take no notice** (*of* s.o./sth)
not to be influenced by someone or something; to ignore

She took no notice of my warning./I'm not going to take any notice of their criticism.

3 **to pay no attention** (*to* s.o./sth)
to take no notice of someone or something; to behave as if someone or something is unimportant

She paid no attention to my point of view./Pay no attention to him – he doesn't know what he's talking about.

4 **to disregard** (sth)
to ignore

Disregard what I told you before – the situation is different now.

5 **regardless** (*of* s.o./sth)
without paying any attention to someone or something

I'm going to do it regardless of what anyone thinks.

Unit 48 Exercises

48.1 *The word in capitals at the end of each of the following sentences can be used to form a word that fits suitably in the blank space. Fill each blank in this way.*

EXAMPLE We had an interesting *discussion* about football.   DISCUSS

1 He completely .... the signs telling him to slow down, and ended up crashing into a wall.   REGARD

2 Her words made a great .... on the crowd.   IMPRESS

3 Your personal experiences have a .... on your attitude to life.   BEAR

4 He pays no .... to anything I say.   ATTEND

5 She's determined to prove his innocence, ... of how long it takes.   REGARD

48.2 *For each of the sentences below, write a new sentence as similar as possible in meaning to the original sentence, but using the word given. This word must not be altered in any way.*

EXAMPLE   It's no use arguing: I've made up my mind.
           point

ANSWER   *There's no point in arguing; I've made up my mind.*

1 Don't listen to him – he doesn't know what he's talking about.
   notice

   ....

2 Your mistake didn't influence the way things turned out.
   difference

   ....

3 The recent increases in air fares haven't changed the number of people wanting to fly.
   effect

   ....

4 We all felt sad at the news of her death.
   affected

   ....

5 He was partly responsible for his own failure.
   contributed

   ....

6 I don't influence the way that the business is managed.
   say

   ....

7 Don't let other people have an effect on you!
   influenced

   ....

8 Everyone contributed to the team's success.
   part

   ....

9 His personal problems have an influence on his ability to do his job.
   affect

   ....

10 I didn't react to his unpleasant comments.
    ignored

    ....

11 A lot of people believe that television affects the way we behave.
    influence

    ....

Unit 49 Involve/Interfere

Part 1

1 **to involve**
   a (sth/*doing* sth)
   to require or include as a
   necessary part or consequence

   *The job involves a lot of travel./Having a party involves
   inviting people, buying food .../I won't accept the offer
   until I know what's involved.*

   b (s.o. *in* sth)
   to become or cause to become
   part of something

   *Don't involve yourself in their problems./We didn't tell you
   because we didn't want to involve you.*

2 **involved**
   a (*in* sth)
   having an active part in something

   *He's involved in various different kinds of business./It's
   impossible to get anything done as there are just too many
   people involved.*

   b (*with* s.o.)
   closely connected or in a close
   relationship with someone

   *Don't get involved with him – he's dishonest./She's
   seriously involved with a married man.*

3 **involvement** (*in* sth)
   the act of being involved

   His involvement in politics began when he was a student.

4 **to mean** (*doing* sth)
   to involve as a necessary
   consequence

   Starting a business means taking a risk.

5 **to take part** (*in* sth)
   to participate in or be part of (an
   organised event etc.)

   Thousands of people took part in the demonstration.

6 **to join**
   a (sth)
   to become a member

   I joined a union when I started work.

   b (s.o.)
   to come together with

   Why don't you join us for dinner tonight?

7 **to join in** (*with* s.o.)
   to start doing what other people
   are doing

   Everybody else was singing so I joined in (with them).

8 **to go along/come along**
   to go or come with someone; to
   accompany someone

   *They were going to a party, so I went along too./We're
   going to the pub tonight. Why don't you come along?*

9 **to concern** (s.o.)
   to affect or involve; to be of
   interest or importance to someone

   *I don't want to hear your opinion – this situation doesn't
   concern you./The environment is an issue which concerns
   us all.*

10 **to interfere**
to get involved in something that doesn't concern you

I wish you'd stop interfering! This is my business.

11 **interference**
the act of interfering

I could do this a lot faster without your interference.

12 **to be nosey**
to be too interested in other people's private matters

She's terribly nosey – she's always asking personal questions.

13 **to pry** (*into* sth)
to try to find out about someone's personal, private life

I don't like to pry but who was that man I saw you with last night?/I hate these forms which pry into your financial affairs.

14 **to gatecrash** (sth)
to go (to a party, concert etc.) without an invitation/ticket

A lot of people gatecrashed the party.

15 **to have nothing to do with** (s.o.)
not to concern someone

This has got nothing to do with you, so don't interfere.

16 **to be none of your business**
not to concern you

I'm not going to say anything about it, because it's none of my business./'How much do you earn, Dad?' – 'That's none of your business.'

17 **to mind your own business**
not to interfere

Mind your own business! This is a private matter.

18 **to keep out** (*of* sth)
not to get involved in something

I kept out of their argument because it had nothing to do with me.

19 **to keep yourself to yourself**
to stay on your own; not to get involved with people

The neighbours hardly know him because he keeps himself to himself.

20 **to keep your distance** (*from* s.o.)
not to get involved with someone

I'm keeping my distance from him because I don't trust him.

21 **to keep someone at arm's length**
not to get too involved or friendly with someone

She kept him at arm's length for the first couple of months until she was completely sure that she could trust him.

Unit 49 Exercises

49.1 *Choose the word or phrase (A, B, C or D) which best completes each sentence.*

1 I've .... a sports club so that I can play regularly.
  A joined   B enlisted   C taken part in   D involved

2 Stop .... ! This has nothing to do with you.
  A gatecrashing   B interfering   C involving   D introducing

3 My previous job involved .... the office.
  A run   B to run   C running   D that I ran

4 You go ahead to the restaurant. I'll .... you later.
  A join   B unite with   C come along with   D accompany

5 We're going for a drink now – why don't you ....
  A join   B come with   C come along   D accompany

49.2 *The word in capitals at the end of each of the following sentences can be used to form a word that fits suitably in the blank space. Fill each blank in this way.*

EXAMPLE We had an interesting *discussion* about football.   DISCUSS

1 Reports suggest the .... of a senior minister in the scandal.   INVOLVE

2 Leave me alone! I don't want any ....   INTERFERE

3 Don't be so .... !   NOSE

4 He stood at the door to make sure that no one .... the party.   GATE

5 We never intended to get so .... with each other.   INVOLVE

49.3 *Fill each of the blanks with one suitable word.*

1 I never wanted to involve you .... my problems.

2 .... your own business – this has got nothing to do with you.

3 I asked if I could join .... with their game.

4 After her refusal of marriage, he resolved to keep her at .... length.

5 My private life is .... of your business.

6 She prefers to .... herself to herself.

49.4 *For each of the sentences below, write a new sentence as similar as possible in meaning to the original sentence, but using the word given. This word must not be altered in any way.*

EXAMPLE   It's no use arguing: I've made up my mind.
          point

ANSWER   *There's no point in arguing; I've made up my mind.*

1 I wish he wouldn't keep asking me about my sex life.
  prying

  ....

212

2 If you have children, you have to change your whole lifestyle.
   means

   ....

3 This is none of your business.
   concern

   ....

4 I didn't get involved in their conversation.
   kept

   ....

5 She said it was none of my business.
   nothing

   ....

6 I prefer not to get too involved with him.
   distance

   ....

7 I didn't participate in the argument.
   part

   ....

8 The decision had nothing to do with me.
   involved

   ....

Unit 50 Succeed/Fail

Part 1

1 **to succeed**
   a (*in doing* sth)
   to do what you have tried to do;
   to reach your aim

   He tried to persuade me but he didn't succeed./After months of planning and several attempts, the two men finally succeeded in climbing Mount Everest.

   b to have the result that was intended or wished for; to work in a satisfactory way

   If their plan had succeeded, the robbers would have got away with more than £5,000,000./Nobody really expects their marriage to succeed.

   c to do well in life; to reach a high position

   She started her career, determined to succeed.

2 **successful** (*in doing* sth)
   having succeeded in what you wanted to do or in what was intended

   I hope you'll be successful in finding somewhere to live./It was a successful evening and everyone enjoyed themselves./She's a successful actress.

3 **success**
   the act of succeeding; the achievement of wealth, fame etc.

   He works hard because he wants success.

4 **a success**
   a successful person or thing

   The meal was a success – everyone liked it./Now that he's such a success on television, he never sees his old friends.

5 **to make a success of** (sth)
   to make sure that something is successful

   She's determined to make a success of the business.

6 **to manage** (*to do* sth)
   to succeed in doing something difficult

   I looked for the book in several shops but I didn't manage to find it./Did you manage to find your keys?

7 **to achieve** (sth)
   to succeed in reaching your aim

   She's always wanted to be rich and now she's achieved it.

8 **an achievement**
   something that is achieved, especially by hard work, effort and perseverance

   The fact that she got an A in the exam, despite all her family problems, is a wonderful achievement.

9 **to make progress**
   to move forwards towards achieving something

   He understood virtually nothing at the beginning of the course, but he's making progress now.

10 **to get somewhere**
   to make progress

   After years of struggling to make his company profitable, he's finally getting somewhere.

11 **to make headway**
   to make progress with a problem or difficult situation

   There's still a lot of work to do on the house, but we're making headway.

12 **to do well**
to achieve success; to make progress

She's doing well at school and getting high marks in all her exams.

13 **to go places**
to become more and more successful in your career

She's very ambitious and I'm sure that whatever she chooses to do, she'll go places.

14 **to make it**
to become successful in achieving what you want

After years of trying he finally made it as a professional musician./She wants to be a doctor but I don't think she'll make it.

15 **to fulfil your potential**
to achieve the success that you are capable of

As a young woman she was considered to have a brilliant future, but she never quite fulfilled her potential.

16 **to realise** (sth)
to succeed in making something (a hope, ambition etc.) real

She finally realised her ambition to travel round the world.

17 **a hit**
a successful film, play or record etc.

This record was a hit a few years ago.

18 **to get your own way**
to succeed in getting what you want despite opposition and often selfishly

I insisted for so long, that I eventually got my own way.

Part 2

1 **to fail**
a (*to do* sth)
not to succeed

America's latest attempt on the world land speed record has failed./She failed to convince the jury of her innocence./She asked a lot of questions but she failed to find out what his secret was.

b (sth)
not to pass (a test or examination)

'How did you get on in your Biology exam?' – 'Oh, I failed.'

2 **failure**
the act of failing; a lack of success

The peace talks seem almost certain to end in failure.

3 **a failure**
an unsuccessful person or thing

The film has been a complete box-office failure./He gets depressed because he thinks he's a failure.

4 **unsuccessful**
not successful

I applied for a job but I was unsuccessful.

5 **to come to nothing**
(of a plan, opportunity etc.) to fail
to happen; to result in nothing

I thought he was going to give me a job but the offer came to nothing.

6 **to fall through**
(of a plan, business deal etc.) to
fail to happen or be completed
successfully

The trip to France fell through at the last minute because I broke my leg./The deal fell through.

7 **to get nowhere**
to make no progress

I've been trying to repair this car for ages but I'm getting nowhere./No matter how much I tried to convince him, I didn't get anywhere.

8 **to draw a blank**
to fail to find what you are
looking for

I phoned several agencies for a ticket but drew a blank at all of them.

9 **at a standstill**
not progressing

Her career is at a standstill at the moment and she's frustrated.

10 **to fall back on** (sth)
to have available in case
something else fails

My father insisted that I got some qualifications so that I would have something to fall back on in case I didn't make it as an actor.

Part 3

1 **to go well**
(of an event or situation etc.) to be
successful; to progress
successfully

The party went well – everyone enjoyed it./'How's your new job?' – 'Oh, it's going really well.'

2 **to go smoothly**
to go well and be free of
problems

The journey went very smoothly and we arrived with time to spare.

3 **to go according to plan**
(of an event or situation etc.) to
progress in the way that was
planned

If everything goes according to plan, I'll be travelling the world next year.

4 **to work**
(of a plan or idea etc.) to succeed

It's a good idea but I don't think it'll work./I tried to persuade him but it didn't work.

5 **to go wrong**
to start happening in a way that
was unplanned and to begin to fail

Whenever things go wrong, he runs to his parents.

6 **to go badly**
(of an event or situation etc.) to be
unsuccessful

The exam went badly because I couldn't answer any of the questions.

Unit 50 Exercises

50.1 *Choose the word or phrase (A, B, C or D) which best completes each sentence.*

1 She never really .... it as an actress.
  A made   B fulfilled   C got   D managed

2 If our plan .... , we'll have the money by Friday.
  A goes   B functions   C achieves   D works

3 She's .... well at work and should get promoted soon.
  A going   B doing   C making   D getting

4 After several months of hard work, the police are finally .... somewhere with their investigation.
  A going   B doing   C making   D getting

5 Our plans to have a party fell .... when Mum and Dad came back a week early from holiday.
  A down   B back   C out   D through

6 She gave up arguing with him because she wasn't .... anything.
  A fulfilling   B making   C achieving   D managing

7 He .... his ambition to be famous.
  A managed   B realised   C won   D succeeded

8 The group had a .... once, but none of their other songs was successful.
  A win   B hit   C success   D achievement

50.2 *The word in capitals at the end of each of the following sentences can be used to form a word that fits suitably in the blank space. Fill each blank in this way.*

EXAMPLE We had an interesting *discussion* about football.   DISCUSS

1 I hope the meeting was ....   SUCCEED

2 Landing a spacecraft on the moon was a great .... for mankind.   ACHIEVE

3 He may be a very good actor, but as a singer he is a complete ....   FAIL

4 Her business has been a huge ....   SUCCEED

5 The negotiations are at a .... , with neither side willing to make concessions. STAND

6 Despite going to German classes twice a week, I don't feel I'm making much .... with the language.   HEAD

7 His attempt to break the world record was sadly ....   SUCCEED

50.3 *Fill each of the blanks with one suitable word.*

1 Decorating the house is a big job, but we're .... progress.

2 Attempts by the police to find him have all drawn a ....

3 He did so little work that it's hardly surprising that he .... all of his exams.

4 It's nice to know that I've got my old job to fall .... if my new one goes badly.

5 I feel sorry for her that all her efforts have .... to nothing.

6 She's an excellent student and we all hope she will .... her potential in the years to come.

7 His last three marriages have ended in divorce, but he's determined to .... a success of this one.

8 Despite working all through the night she .... to finish the job on time.

50.4 *For each of the sentences below, write a new sentence as similar as possible in meaning to the original sentence, but using the word given. This word must not be altered in any way.*

     EXAMPLE   It's no use arguing: I've made up my mind.
               point
     ANSWER   *There's no point in arguing; I've made up my mind.*

1 Was the exam OK?
well

   ....

2 Although I set off late, I succeeded in getting there on time.
managed

   ....

3 Nothing bad happened on my first day at work.
smoothly

   ....

4 The whole day happened as planned.
according

   ....

5 I gave up trying to make friends with the other students because I was making no progress.
nowhere

   ....

6 It seems that whatever I try to do, something bad always happens.
wrong

   ....

7 She always gets what she wants.
way

   ....

8 He's becoming very successful.
places

   ....

9 Did you manage to get a ticket?
succeed

   ....

10 The evening was unsuccessful and ended in an argument.
badly

   ....

Appendix Irregular verbs

Infinitive	Past tense	Past participle	Infinitive	Past tense	Past participle
arise	arose	arisen	get	got	got
awake	awoke	awoken, awaked	give	gave	given
be (am, is, are)	was, were	been	go	went	gone
bear	bore	borne	grind	ground	ground
beat	beat	beaten	grow	grew	grown
become	became	become	hang	hung	hung
begin	began	begun	have (has)	had	had
bend	bent	bent	hear	heard	heard
bet	bet	bet	hide	hid	hidden
bid	bid	bid	hit	hit	hit
bind	bound	bound	hold	held	held
bite	bit	bitten	hurt	hurt	hurt
bleed	bled	bled	keep	kept	kept
blow	blew	blown	kneel	knelt	knelt
break	broke	broken	know	knew	known
breed	bred	bred	lay	laid	laid
bring	brought	brought	lead	led	led
broadcast	broadcast	broadcast	lean	leant, leaned	leant, leaned
build	built	built	leap	leapt, leaped	leapt, leaped
burn	burnt, burned	burnt, burned	learn	learnt, learned	learnt, learned
burst	burst	burst	leave	left	left
buy	bought	bought	lend	lent	lent
cast	cast	cast	let	let	let
catch	caught	caught	lie	lay	lain
choose	chose	chosen	light	lit	lit
cling	clung	clung	lose	lost	lost
come	came	come	make	made	made
cost	cost	cost	mean	meant	meant
creep	crept	crept	meet	met	met
cut	cut	cut	mistake	mistook	mistaken
deal	dealt	dealt	misunderstand	misunderstood	misunderstood
dig	dug	dug	pay	paid	paid
do	did	done	put	put	put
draw	drew	drawn	read	read	read
dream	dreamt, dreamed	dreamt, dreamed	ride	rode	ridden
drink	drank	drunk	ring	rang, rung	rung
drive	drove	driven	rise	rose	risen
eat	ate	eaten	run	ran	run
fall	fell	fallen	say	said	said
feed	fed	fed	see	saw	seen
feel	felt	felt	seek	sought	sought
fight	fought	fought	sell	sold	sold
find	found	found	send	sent	sent
flee	fled	fled	set	set	set
fling	flung	flung	sew	sewed	sewn, sewed
fly	flew	flown	shake	shook	shaken
forbid	forbade, forbad	forbidden	shine	shone	shone
forecast	forecast	forecast	shoot	shot	shot
foresee	foresaw	foreseen	show	showed	shown, showed
forget	forgot	forgotten	shrink	shrank	shrunk
forgive	forgave	forgiven	shut	shut	shut
freeze	froze	frozen	sing	sang	sung

Infinitive	Past tense	Past participle
sink	sank	sunk, sunken
sit	sat	sat
slay	slew	slain
sleep	slept	slept
slide	slid	slid
slit	slit	slit
smell	smelt, smelled	smelt, smelled
sow	sowed	sown, sowed
speak	spoke	spoken
speed	sped	sped
spell	spelt, spelled	spelt, spelled
spend	spent	spent
spill	spilt, spilled	spilt, spilled
spin	spun, span	spun
spit	spat	spat
split	split	split
spoil	spoilt, spoiled	spoilt, spoiled
spread	spread	spread
spring	sprang	sprung
stand	stood	stood
steal	stole	stolen
stick	stuck	stuck
sting	stung	stung
stink	stank, stunk	stunk
strike	struck	struck, stricken
swear	swore	sworn
sweep	swept	swept
swim	swam	swum
swing	swung	swung
take	took	taken
teach	taught	taught
tear	tore	torn
tell	told	told
think	thought	thought
throw	threw	thrown
thrust	thrust	thrust
tread	trod	trodden, trod
understand	understood	understood
unwind	unwound	unwound
upset	upset	upset
wake	woke	woken
wear	wore	worn
weave	wove	woven
weep	wept	wept
win	won	won
wind	wound	wound
write	wrote	written

Answer Key

Unit 1

1.1 1B 2D 3D 4C 5D 6B 7A 8B
9C 10D 11B 12A 13C 14D 15D
16A 17D 18A 19C

1.2 1 Use 2 about/around 3 good 4 make
5 around 6 up 7 about 8 on

Unit 2

2.1 1D 2A 3D 4D 5A 6B 7B 8D
9C 10A 11D 12C 13D 14A 15D
16A 17B 18C 19C 20D 21C
22C 23C 24A 25D

2.2 1 Take care of yourself.
2 Watch out for thieves if you go to that
part of town.
3 I took a lot of trouble over this letter.
4 I've installed an alarm to protect my
car from/against thieves.
5 I bought it on the spur of the moment.
6 You're jumping to conclusions.
7 I'm very particular about who I discuss
my private life with.
8 I was careful not to offend them.
9 I'll keep my eyes open for you at the
concert, although I expect it will be
very crowded.
10 She's very fussy about the kind of
hotels she stays in.
11 Will you look after the flat while I'm
away?
12 Mind your head!/Mind you don't hit
your head!
13 I'm not fussy whether we go or not.
14 Look out for a red door when you
arrive – that's my flat.

Unit 3

3.1 1C 2C 3B 4D 5C 6C 7A 8A
9B 10C

3.2 1 You're not telling the truth.
2 To be honest, I didn't understand a
word he said.
3 Is she trustworthy?
4 To be frank, you're wasting your time.
5 He's never afraid to speak his mind.
6 The witness is completely reliable.
7 To tell you the truth, I couldn't care
less what you think.

8 Frankly, there's no easy solution to
your problems.

Unit 4

4.1 1C 2D 3B 4C 5C 6A 7D 8B
9A 10A 11B 12D 13D 14B 15C
16A 17B

4.2 1 rip 2 about 3 liar 4 cheat 5 lie

4.3 1 He conned me into paying far too
much for it.
2 Why are you lying to me?
3 She tricked me into giving her £10./
She tricked me out of £10.
4 I told a lie because I didn't want to say
what had really happened.
5 They ripped me off.
6 When I checked my change, I realised
that I'd been done out of £5.
7 He conned me out of a lot of money./
He conned me into giving him a lot of
money.
8 He cheated me out of £20.
9 You weren't taken in by his story, were
you?

Unit 5

5.1 1B 2C 3B 4C 5D 6C 7A 8A
9C 10B 11C 12D

5.2 1 selfishness 2 appreciation 3 unkind
4 consideration 5 sympathetic 6 greed
7 kindness 8 appreciative

5.3 1 give 2 with 3 tight 4 grateful
5 appreciate 6 for 7 self 8 greedy

Unit 6

6.1 1A 2C 3B 4A 5C 6B 7C 8B
9D 10B 11C 12B 13B 14A 15A
16C

6.2 1 offence 2 tactful 3 flattery
4 crawler 5 well-mannered 6 offensive
7 tactless 8 ill-mannered/bad-mannered

6.3 1 insult 2 flattering 3 cheek
4 compliment 5 flattered 6 offended
7 tact

Unit 7

7.1　1D　2B　3A　4B　5C　6B　7D　8B
　　9C　10A

7.2　1 self-conscious　2 boast/brag　3 bossy
　　4 modest　5 self-confidence　6 show off
　　7 condescending/patronising
　　8 big-headed　9 down to　10 confident
　　11 domineering　12 below/beneath
　　13 self-confident　14 down on
　　15 boasting/bragging about
　　16 confidence

Unit 8

8.1　1C　2A　3A　4D　5B　6C　7A　8B

8.2　1 pig-headed　2 determination
　　3 persistence　4 perseverance
　　5 single-minded

8.3　1 take no　2 to　3 in　4 set in　5 at
　　6 with

Unit 9

9.1　1C　2D　3A　4B　5C　6B

9.2　1 impatient　2 intolerance
　　3 broad-minded　4 patience　5 tolerant

9.3　1 patient　2 up with　3 stand
　　4 intolerant　5 tolerate　6 tolerance

Unit 10

10.1　1B　2C　3D　4B　5D　6C　7B　8C
　　9B　10C　11A

10.2　1 frustrating　2 irritable　3 annoying
　　4 frustration　5 irritating　6 infuriating

10.3　1 She'll go mad when she finds out
　　　what's happened.
　　2 He lost his temper because we all
　　　disagreed with him.
　　3 She's in a bad mood today.
　　4 I'm sick (and tired) of being treated as
　　　an inferior!
　　5 He had a fit when he saw the damage
　　　that had been done to his car.
　　6 His arrogance gets up my nose.
　　7 I've had enough of people ordering me
　　　about.
　　8 Waiting for buses gets on my nerves.
　　9 Having to get up so early is a pain in
　　　the neck.

10　It makes me sick to see so much food
　　being wasted.

Unit 11

11.1　1A　2A　3A　4C　5B

11.2　1 sure/certain　2 optimist　3 of
　　4 pessimist　5 doubts

11.3　1 Hopefully, I'll be going/I'm going
　　　skiing at Christmas.
　　2 I'm sceptical of/about his reasons for
　　　being nice to me.
　　3 Look on the bright side! You're young
　　　and healthy and will have plenty more
　　　opportunities.
　　4 Are you optimistic about your chances
　　　of getting promotion?
　　5 I'm not quite sure of/about the meaning
　　　of this word.
　　6 All I can do is cross my fingers and
　　　hope for the best.
　　7 No doubt he'll be late, as usual.
　　8 I'm pessimistic about the future.
　　9 I had (my) reservations about him at
　　　first, but now he seems very good at
　　　his job.
　　10 Is she hopeful of getting the job?

Unit 12

12.1　1C　2A　3A　4D　5B　6B

12.2　1 mysterious　2 confusion　3 puzzling
　　4 bewildered　5 confusing　6 mystified

12.3　1 If you change all the plans now, you'll
　　　only cause confusion.
　　2 The whole subject bewilders me.
　　3 What puzzles me is why he did such a
　　　strange thing./It puzzles me why he did
　　　such a strange thing.
　　4 I'm confused about what you want me
　　　to do.
　　5 They look so alike that it's easy to mix
　　　her up with her sister.
　　6 I was so worried that I couldn't think
　　　straight.
　　7 His disappearance is a mystery to us.
　　8 You're not the first person to confuse
　　　me with my twin brother.
　　9 I'm not clear about how to fill in this
　　　form.

Unit 13

13.1 1A 2C 3B 4D 5C 6B 7D 8B
9A 10D 11B 12D

13.2 1 The news of his death hasn't sunk in yet.
2 There are a few problems which we ought to try to clear up.
3 It's obvious that she doesn't like me.
4 He's got such a strong accent that half the time I can't make out a word he's saying.
5 He gave us so much information that it was impossible to take everything in.
6 He obviously doesn't understand you./ Obviously he doesn't understand you.
7 Are you clear about how to find my house?

Unit 14

14.1 1 humiliation 2 embarrassed
3 shame 4 embarrassment
5 humiliated 6 embarrassing
7 humiliating 8 guilt

14.2 1 about 2 of 3 make 4 blushed
5 about

14.3 1 Things have got so bad that I'm reduced to having to borrow money from other people.
2 I felt a fool when I realised what I'd done.
3 Her lack of education is an embarrassment to her.
4 She went red at the mention of his name.
5 He feels responsible for the accident.
6 He's got a (guilty) conscience about cheating them.
7 It embarrasses her when people tell her how beautiful she is.
8 The boss likes to humiliate people in front of others.

Unit 15

15.1 1D 2C 3B 4C 5B 6C 7C 8C
9A 10C 11B 12C 13A 14B 15A
16B 17D

15.2 1 I didn't dare (to) tell him what I really thought.

2 Some people are frightened to go out because of the amount of crime.
3 I'm afraid of him.
4 I said nothing for fear of offending her.
5 They have three locks on the door because they're afraid of being burgled.
6 I'm dreading making that speech at the wedding tomorrow.
7 I agreed with him because I was scared of making the situation even worse.
8 I don't know what's going to happen but I fear the worst.
9 I'm being very careful because I'm frightened of making a mistake.
10 It's a frightening thought.
11 I dread to think how much it's going to cost.
12 When I think what the world might be like in twenty years' time it scares me./ It scares me to think what the world might be like in twenty years' time.
13 I wouldn't have the nerve to say a thing like that.
14 I'm terrified of guns.

Unit 16

16.1 1C 2A 3B 4B 5C 6D

16.2 1 enjoyable 2 satisfactory
3 willingness 4 thrilling 5 enjoyment
6 delightful 7 satisfaction 8 exciting
9 pleasure 10 excitement 11 happiness

16.3 1 with 2 for 3 about 4 about 5 for

16.4 1 I hope you enjoy yourself.
2 I bought myself a present to cheer myself up.
3 I'm willing to discuss it with you.
4 Did you have a good time last night?
5 I'm happy to do whatever you want me to do.
6 I enjoyed seeing all my old friends again.
7 I'm prepared to work hard, if that's what I have to do.
8 Are you pleased with your new car?
9 She won't be happy about me changing the arrangements.
10 I'm looking forward to seeing you next week.

Unit 17

17.1 1C 2C 3D 4D 5C 6B 7B

17.2 1 about 2 in/with 3 about 4 up
5 about/at

17.3 1 hurtful 2 upsetting 3 depressing
4 sadness 5 depression 6 reluctance
7 disappointing 8 unhappiness
9 depressed 10 miserable

17.4 1 If you want to make a complaint, you'll
have to see the manager.
2 I'm reluctant to criticise him because
he's a good friend of mine.
3 When I was away, I missed my family.
4 Her job is getting her down.
5 We were expecting her to win, so it
was a disappointment when she didn't.

Unit 18

18.1 1C 2C 3C 4A 5C 6B

18.2 1 enthusiasm 2 fascinating
3 boredom 4 interest 5 fanatics
6 obsession 7 bore 8 interests

18.3 1 I was fascinated by the stories she told
me.
2 He sounded (as if he was) enthusiastic
about staying with us for the weekend.
3 He's more interested in making money
than anything else.
4 I'm bored with this programme; let's
watch something else.
5 I would be interested to know why it
happened.
6 Things bore her very quickly.
7 Is there anything in that magazine that
interests you?
8 Grammar exercises bore me stiff.
9 I'm fed up with going to the same
places all the time.

Unit 19

19.1 1A 2D 3C 4C 5C 6D 7B

19.2 1 envied 2 Jealousy 3 resentment
4 spiteful 5 bitterness 6 envy

19.3 1 She resents being treated like the office
slave.

2 He's got a chip on his shoulder because
he didn't go to university.
3 He got his own back on her.
4 They're resentful about not getting paid
what they think they should be paid.
5 I don't begrudge her her success (– she
deserves it).
6 I'm envious of their happy relationship.

Unit 20

20.1 1 feel ... for 2 about/for 3 made ...
excuse 4 apology 5 apologise 6 for

20.2 1 I'm afraid (that) I'm rather busy at the
moment.
2 He apologised for not telling me before.
3 I was sorry to leave that house because
I liked living there.
4 We regret that we won't be able to
come to your party.
5 I'm sorry to (have to) inform you that
we no longer need you.

Unit 21

21.1 1D 2C 3A 4C 5A 6C 7C 8A
9C 10B 11B 12C 13C 14A 15C
16B 17B 18C 19A 20C 21A

21.2 1 The offer to go and work in Brazil
came (completely) out of the blue.
2 It comes as no surprise to me that he's
got money problems.
3 No wonder he looks so miserable –
I've just found out that he's lot his job.
4 The sudden noise made me jump.
5 His rudeness took me aback./I was
taken aback by his rudeness.
6 It isn't easy to shock me./I'm not easy
to shock.
7 You caught me unawares, so I haven't
tidied the house yet.
8 I was so surprised that I was
speechless.
9 It came as/was a shock to me when my
friends suddenly decided to leave the
country.

Unit 22

22.1 1D 2A 3B 4A 5A 6B 7C 8D
9A 10C

22.2 1 I could do with an early night.

2 She criticised me for leaving early.
3 He's crazy about cars.
4 I don't feel like going to that party tonight.
5 She's got a low opinion of politicians.
6 I fancy going somewhere else for a change.
7 A lot of men disapprove of women working.
8 I'm desperate for a holiday.

22.3 1 to 2 up 3 down 4 on 5 off

22.4 1 She's fond of children.
2 I wasn't in the mood for a serious conversation.
3 They've got good taste in furniture.
4 I'm not really keen on this kind of music.
5 They were full of praise for your cooking.
6 She's critical of other people's weaknesses.
7 I have a lot of affection for her.
8 I'm keen to learn as much as I can.
9 They've been raving about the hotel.
10 She thinks highly of you.
11 I don't approve of violence in any circumstances.
12 I'm dying to see her again.
13 I think a lot of him.
14 I think that the film is overrated.
15 I didn't think much of the restaurant.
16 She despises him.

Unit 23
23.1 1C 2D 3B 4B 5C 6A 7A 8C
9C 10C 11A 12C 13C 14B 15C
16A 17C 18D 19A 20B 21B
22C 23B 24C 25A 26D

23.2 1 ease 2 up 3 under 4 on
5 nerve 6 about

Unit 24
24.1 1B 2A 3C 4C 5C 6B 7C 8D
9D 10B 11D

24.2 1 comfortable 2 relieved 3 reassure/ assure 4 relaxation 5 comforting

24.3 1 Her friends' messages of sympathy were a comfort to her during her illness.
2 Please make yourself at home.
3 He takes everything in his stride.
4 Why don't you take it easy for a few days and let me look after the shop?
5 She breathed a sigh of relief when she realised that her bag hadn't been stolen.

Unit 25
25.1 1B 2B 3B 4D 5D 6C 7C 8A
9B

25.2 1 Adverts tempt people into spending more than they can afford.
2 She is attracted to older men.
3 I was tempted to walk out without paying because the service was so bad.
4 Their lifestyle appeals to me, although I probably wouldn't really enjoy it.
5 I couldn't resist the temptation to buy the dress.
6 I can't see the attraction of spending all day on the beach.

Unit 26
26.1 1C 2C 3C 4B 5B 6D 7B 8A
9C 10C

26.2 1 When she left home, she had to fend for herself.
2 If you leave this job, don't count on getting another one.
3 I may go out tonight, depending on how long my homework takes me.
4 I'm banking on being promoted soon.
5 Most university students depend on the financial support of their parents.
6 If I were you, I wouldn't rely on the weather being good.
7 I built this on my own.
8 I want to be free to enjoy myself.
9 I don't want to be dependent on other people.
10 They rely on her income.
11 Our car is extremely reliable; it hasn't let us down once in the last ten years.

Unit 27

27.1 1B 2D 3D 4B 5B 6C 7C 8B
     9D 10A 11B

27.2 1 I can't tell the difference between the original painting and the copy.
2 I don't want to split hairs, but your facts aren't quite right.
3 What he earns in a week is equivalent to/is the equivalent of what I earn in a month.
4 The way he behaves in private contrasts with the way he behaves at work.
5 This record is no different to/from the last one they made.
6 Parents try to teach their children to distinguish between right and wrong.
7 This programme is similar to one that used to be on years ago.
8 I prefer playing football, as opposed to watching it.
9 There is a subtle difference between being mean and being careful with money.
10 Not having much money is different to/from being completely broke.
11 There has been a difference in his attitude recently.
12 Some people say that there's a thin line between love and hate.

Unit 28

28.1 1 acquaintance 2 old 3 colleagues
     4 good/close 5 best 6 friendship

28.2 1 I'm on good terms with everyone at work.
2 We got to know each other during the journey.
3 She gets on (well) with most people.
4 Have you made friends with anyone since you arrived?
5 He's fallen out with Clare.
6 Have you heard the news? Roger and Diana have split up./Roger has split up with Diana.
7 He's been going out with her for about three weeks./They've been going out (together) for about three weeks.
8 They broke up last month.
9 I used to be friends with him.

Unit 29

29.1 1C 2B 3A 4B 5A 6B

29.2 1 punch 2 out 3 sense
     4 played ... on 5 fun 6 told

29.3 1 You know I told you I was a millionaire? Well, I was pulling your leg.
2 Her jokes were very funny.
3 Everybody laughed at him because he didn't know the answer.
4 Her comments were (very) witty.
5 You're kidding. He's not really your brother, is he?
6 It's a brilliant film – I laughed my head off all the way through.
7 She obviously wasn't amused by your jokes.
8 Everybody took the mickey out of him because he'd had his hair cut so short.
9 I found her story hysterical.

Unit 30

30.1 1B 2D 3C 4C 5D 6A 7B 8B
     9C 10D 11D

30.2 1 off 2 down 3 above
     4 down 5 what

30.3 1 Don't you understand the importance of being more careful?
2 He stressed that it was only his opinion.
3 I wish you'd take this seriously.
4 What was the significance of his silence?
5 He laughed off his latest business failure.
6 He lives for football.
7 I don't feel (very) strongly about religion.
8 It's vital that you see a doctor as soon as possible.
9 I want to emphasise that I'm not criticising you.
10 It's time you got your priorities right.
11 He made light of the crisis.

Unit 31

31.1 1C 2C 3D 4B 5D 6B 7C 8B
     9C 10C 11D

31.2 1 luckily 2 unfortunate 3 lucky
    4 unfortunately 5 unluckiest 6 fortunate

31.3 1 I bumped into some old friends in the
      pub.
    2 Their party coincides with another one
      I've been invited to.
    3 I happened to be there when she
      revealed the truth.
    4 With a bit of luck, I'll get a job as
      soon as I get there.
    5 Guess who I ran into on my way here?
    6 By a stroke of luck, the boat hadn't
      left.
    7 All being well, I'll see you next week.

Unit 32
32.1 1C 2A 3C 4C 5A 6C 7C 8C
    9C 10A 11C 12C 13B 14C 15D
    16C 17C 18C 19C 20B 21D
    22B 23A 24B 25C

Unit 33
33.1 1D 2D 3A 4A 5A 6C 7B 8C
    9C 10C 11B 12D 13A 14D

33.2 1 hardship 2 millionaire 3 wealthy
    4 poverty 5 luxurious

33.3 1 fortune 2 afford 3 worse 4 owes
    5 debts 6 rolling 7 short

Unit 34
34.1 1B 2A 3A 4D 5B 6A 7C 8C

34.2 1 suit 2 match 3 convenient for
    4 fit 5 inconvenient 6 bad taste
    7 suits 8 convenient for
    9 suitable/right 10 clash

Unit 35
35.1 1A 2C 3D 4A 5A 6A 7A 8B
    9C 10B 11C 12B 13B 14B 15C
    16A 17B 18A 19A 20D 21B
    22B 23B

35.2 1 of 2 to 3 On 4 of 5 to

35.3 1 uncharacteristic 2 remarkable
    3 unreal 4 extraordinary 5 typical

Unit 36
36.1 1 skill 2 flair/gift for 3 up to
    4 talent 5 knack 6 capable 7 flair for

36.2 1 She won't be capable of understanding
      something as difficult as that.
    2 I'm not very good at card games,
      although I can play a bit.
    3 Good advice enabled me to make the
      right decision.
    4 I've tried, but I'm simply no good at
      cooking.
    5 He's hopeless at making decisions.
    6 Swimming came naturally to me.
    7 She's good at explaining things.

Unit 37
37.1 1B 2A 3C 4D 5B 6D 7C 8B
    9A 10D 11C 12A 13B 14C 15D
    16A 17B 18B 19A

37.2 1 anticipation 2 unpredictable
    3 expectations 4 outlook 5 knowing

37.3 1 It remains to be seen whether he'll
      keep his promise or not.
    2 I'm afraid I'll be a bit late because
      something has cropped up.
    3 The result was a foregone conclusion.
    4 What you're doing is potentially
      dangerous.
    5 There's no telling how long it will take
      to do this.
    6 The odds are that nothing will go
      wrong.
    7 The party is in doubt, because she's ill.
    8 He's liable to get here late; he usually
      does.
    9 The potential profit is enormous./There
      is an enormous potential profit.
    10 It's touch and go whether I'll be able
      to pay the bills this month.
    11 I don't anticipate seeing him for some
      time.

Unit 38
38.1 1C 2C 3C 4B 5D 6A 7A 8B
    9B

38.2 1 If you concentrated on your work, you
      might not make so many mistakes.
    2 A lot of things keep getting in the way
      of my work.

3 You'll have to get down to some serious work soon.

4 I'm trying to concentrate, but all that noise you're making is putting me off.

5 I don't like intruding on her when she's busy.

6 Leave me alone! Can't you see I'm working?

7 He's so preoccupied with work at the moment that he doesn't have any time for his family.

Unit 39

39.1 1 You should take the price into consideration/take into consideration the price before you decide whether to buy it or not.

2 He's in two minds about whether to go or not.

3 I've weighed up the pros and cons and I've decided not to go.

4 Bearing in mind that she's only just started, she's doing very well.

5 She's having second thoughts about marrying him now.

6 They will take age and experience into account/take into account age and experience when they decide the salary.

7 I was going to argue with him, but I thought better of it.

8 That suggestion is out./I've ruled out that suggestion.

9 I'm considering leaving the country, but I haven't decided yet.

10 When I agreed to do this, I didn't bargain for it being so expensive.

11 I'm thinking of selling this car and buying another one.

39.2 1 considered 2 think 3 out 4 mind
     5 over 6 for 7 second 8 allowances
     9 changed

Unit 40

40.1 1B 2C 3C 4B 5A 6D 7C 8D
     9D 10B 11A

40.2 1 sensible 2 realistic 3 intelligence
     4 educated 5 practical 6 perceptive

Unit 41

41.1 1C 2C 3D 4B 5C 6A 7A 8B
     9A 10C 11A 12D 13C 14B 15B

41.2 1 foolish 2 idiotic 3 impractical
     4 ridiculous 5 unrealistic

Unit 42

42.1 1A 2D 3D 4A 5D 6C 7B 8C
     9B

42.2 1 slipped 2 left
     3 forgetful/absent-minded
     4 recall/remember 5 back on
     6 by heart 7 minded

42.3 1 I'll make a note of your address in case I need to write to you.

2 Let me jog your memory.

3 I've gone blank.

4 The word is on the tip of my tongue.

5 This song rings a bell.

6 I can't place him.

Unit 43

43.1 1B 2A 3A 4B 5D 6B

43.2 1 gist 2 misunderstood 3 of 4 see
     5 misunderstanding 6 through to

43.3 1 I can't make head or tail of this letter.

2 She's well aware that she will have to work hard.

3 It crossed his mind that he might have misunderstood her.

4 It never occurred to him to tell her.

5 That sentence makes no sense.

6 He was unaware of her feelings for him.

43.4 1 Although I don't speak Italian particularly well, I got her drift.

2 I appreciate that it's not your fault.

3 He's oblivious to what other people are saying about him.

4 I gather from the paper that the economic situation is getting worse.

5 It strikes me that there's only one thing you can do.

6 He wasn't aware of the cost involved in buying a house.

7 After a while it dawned on me that I'd made a terrible mistake.

Unit 44

44.1 1D 2A 3C 4C 5C 6B

44.2 1 contradicted   2 reached
3 compromise   4 accept   5 co-operative
6 accept   7 co-operation
8 controversial   9 with ... about
10 with ... about/on   11 with ... about
12 with

44.3 1 I have no objection to changing my
plans.
2 I thought about it for a while and then
I agreed to their offer.
3 The neighbours were having a row.
4 Are we in agreement?
5 I object to having to pay so much for
so little.
6 He doesn't agree with divorce.
7 I don't want to have an argument with
you.
8 In the end we reached a compromise.
9 I disagree with the way he treats
people.
10 I'll meet you half-way.
11 We've come to an agreement to share
the cost.
12 I expressed my opposition to his plan.
13 He is in favour of capital punishment.
14 If you co-operate with me, everything
will be all right.
15 I never row with my parents.

Unit 45

45.1 1D 2A 3C 4B 5B 6B 7D 8B
9C 10C 11A 12A 13C

45.2 1 out   2 shrugged   3 shake   4 out
5 of   6 nodded   7 to show   8 pulled
9 gesture   10 indication of

Unit 46

46.1 1C 2B 3A 4B 5D 6A

46.2 1 in as/so many   2 warned
3 proposed to   4 implication
5 suggestion   6 Guess   7 advice
8 make

Unit 47

47.1 1 She persuaded me not to leave.
2 He pushed me into buying it.
3 She urged me to think about it
carefully before I decided.
4 She convinced the court that she was
innocent./She convinced the court of
her innocence.
5 She encourages me to make my own
decisions.
6 His wife is pushing him to get a better
job.
7 She persuaded me that I was making a
terrible mistake.
8 What convinced him to go to Italy
instead of France?

47.2 1 on   2 into   3 up   4 off   5 out of

47.3 1 They have security guards to
discourage people from trying to steal/
from stealing.
2 They're putting pressure on me to
make a decision soon.
3 When I make my complaint, I hope
that you'll back me up.
4 She's always trying to impose her
opinions on other people.
5 He has always supported her in her
career.
6 He offered them more money as an
incentive to do the job quickly.
7 The judge gave a harsh sentence to
deter other people from committing the
same crime.
8 Because of the circumstances, I am
forced to act quickly.
9 She was nervous about going to the
doctor's, so I went with her to give her
moral support.
10 He doesn't earn enough money to
support himself.
11 I need as much encouragement as I can
get.
12 Many people believe that the death
penalty is a deterrent.
13 I had no choice but to apologise.
14 I support Hampshire County Cricket
Club.

Unit 48

48.1 1 disregarded   2 impression
      3 bearing   4 attention   5 regardless

48.2 1 Don't take any notice/Take no notice of
        him – he doesn't know what he's
        talking about.
      2 Your mistake didn't make any
        difference/made no difference to the
        way things turned out.
      3 The recent increases in air fares
        haven't had any effect/have had no
        effect on the number of people wanting
        to fly.
      4 We were all affected by the news of
        her death./The news of her death
        affected us all.
      5 He contributed to his own failure.
      6 I don't have a say/I have no say in the
        way that the business is managed.
      7 Don't be influenced by other people!
      8 Everyone played a part in the team's
        success.
      9 His personal problems affect his ability
        to do his job.
     10 I ignored his unpleasant comments.
     11 A lot of people believe that television
        has an influence on the way we behave.

Unit 49

49.1 1A   2B   3C   4A   5C

49.2 1 involvement   2 interference
      3 nosey   4 gatecrashed   5 involved

49.3 1 in   2 Mind   3 in   4 arm's   5 none
      6 keep

49.4 1 I wish he wouldn't keep prying into
        my sex life.
      2 Having children means changing your
        whole lifestyle./If you have children, it
        means changing your whole lifestyle.
      3 This doesn't concern you.
      4 I kept out of their conversation.
      5 She said it had nothing to do with me.
      6 I prefer to keep my distance from him.
      7 I didn't take part in the argument.
      8 I wasn't involved in the decision.

Unit 50

50.1 1A   2D   3B   4D   5D   6C   7B   8B

50.2 1 successful   2 achievement   3 failure
      4 success   5 standstill   6 headway
      7 unsuccessful

50.3 1 making   2 blank   3 failed
      4 back on   5 come   6 fulfil   7 make
      8 failed

50.4 1 Did the exam go well?
      2 Although I set off late, I managed to
        get there on time.
      3 My first day at work went smoothly.
      4 The whole day went according to plan.
      5 I gave up trying to make friends with
        the other students because I was getting
        nowhere.
      6 It seems that whatever I try to do,
        something always goes wrong.
      7 She always gets her own way.
      8 He's going places.
      9 Did you succeed in getting a ticket?
     10 The evening went badly and ended in
        an argument.

Index

The numbers in the index refer to units, not pages.